THE
KIDNEYS
AND THE
RENAL
SYSTEM

THE HUMAN BODY

THE KIDNEYS AND THE RENAL SYSTEM

EDITED BY KARA ROGERS, SENIOR EDITOR, BIOMEDICAL SCIENCES

Educational Publishing

IN ASSOCIATION WITH

EDUCATIONAL SERVICES

Published in 2012 by Britannica Educational Publishing
(a trademark of Encyclopædia Britannica, Inc.)
in association with Rosen Educational Services, LLC
29 East 21st Street, New York, NY 10010.

For a listing of additional Britannica Educational Publishing titles, call toll free (800) 237-9932.

First Edition

Britannica Educational Publishing
Michael I. Levy: Executive Editor
J.E. Luebering: Senior Manager
Adam Augustyn: Assistant Manager
Marilyn L. Barton: Senior Coordinator, Production Control
Steven Bosco: Director, Editorial Technologies
Lisa S. Braucher: Senior Producer and Data Editor
Yvette Charboneau: Senior Copy Editor
Kathy Nakamura: Manager, Media Acquisition
Kara Rogers: Senior Editor, Biomedical Sciences

Rosen Educational Services
Nicholas Croce: Editor
Nelson Sá: Art Director
Cindy Reiman: Photography Manager
Karen Huang: Photo Researcher
Matthew Cauli: Designer, Cover Design
Introduction by Jennifer Capuzzo

Library of Congress Cataloging-in-Publication Data

The kidneys and the renal system/edited by Kara Rogers.—1st ed.
    p. cm.—(The human body)
"In association with Britannica Educational Publishing, Rosen Educational Services."
Includes bibliographical references and index.
ISBN 978-1-61530-679-4 (library binding)
1. Kidneys—Diseases. 2. Kidneys. I. Rogers, Kara.
RC902.K535 2012
616.6'1—dc23

2011026615

Manufactured in the United States of America

On the cover: A 3-dimensional graphic of the kidneys within the body. *Shutterstock.com*

On pages 1, 27, 44, 75, 105, 141, 164, 165, 167, 168: Illustration of the kidneys and renal
system. *Shutterstock.com*

CONTENTS

Introduction   x

Chapter 1: Anatomy of the
Kidneys and Renal System   1
  The Kidneys   1
    Anatomical Location
      of the Kidneys   4
    The Renal Capsule   4
    Renal Vessels and Nerves   5
    Internal Configuration:
      The Renal Pyramid   7
    Internal Configuration:
      The Renal Pelvis   8
    Minute Structure:
      The Nephron and Loop
      of Henle   8
    Minute Structure: The
      Renal Collecting Tubules   12
    Intrarenal Network of
      Blood Vessels   13
  The Ureters   16
    General Characteristics   16
    Structure of the
      Ureteric Wall   16
  The Urinary Bladder   17
    General Description   18
    Blood and Nerve Supplies   19
    Structure of the
      Bladder Wall   20
  The Urethra   21
    General Description   23
    Structure of
      Urethral Wall   24

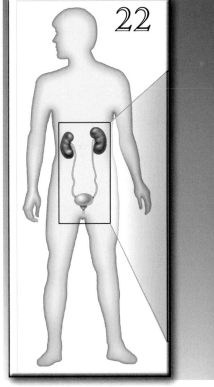

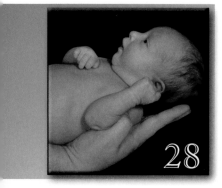

Chapter 2: Development and Function of the Kidneys and Renal System 27

Development of the Renal System 27

Regulatory Functions of the Kidneys 29

Renal Blood Circulation 32

Intrarenal Blood Pressures 33

Factors that Affect Renal Flow 33

Glomerular Pressure 35

The Role of Hormones in Renal Function 36

Biological Considerations 41

Chapter 3: The Physiology of Urinary Excretion 44

Principal Features of Urine and its Excretion 44

Formation and Composition of Urine 48

Relative Composition of Plasma and Urine in Normal Men 48

Glomerular Filtration 49

Tubule Function 51

Effect of Tubular Reabsorption on Urine (Illustrative 24-Hour Figures) 51

Reabsorption from the Proximal Tubule 52

Reabsorption From the Loop of Henle 56

Reabsorption from the Distal Convoluted Tubule 56

The Concentration of Urine 57

Tubular Secretion 60
Regulation of Acid-Base
Balance 61
Volume and Composition
of Urine 64
*Some Urine Constituents
(g/24 Hours)* 65
Urine Collection and
Emission 69
The Bladder 70
   Bladder Function in
   Urination 72
   Neural Control of
   Urination 73

**Chapter 4: Renal Disorders
of Fluid Regulation and
Urinary Function** 75
Effects of Abnormal Renal
Function on Body Fluid 75
Dehydration 80
Diabetes Insipidus 84
Syndrome of Inappropriate
Antidiuretic Hormone 86
Vascular Disease and Renal
Function 88
Disorders of Urine Flow 89
   Obstruction to the Flow
   of Urine 92
   Kidney Stones 95
   Enuresis 96
Urinary Tract Infection 98
   Risk Factors 98
   Causes 100
   Symptoms and
   Diagnosis 100
   Treatment 102

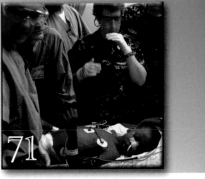

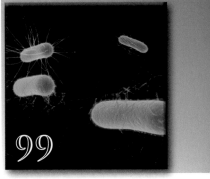

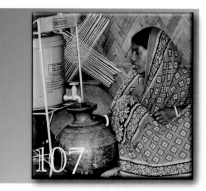

Other Factors in Urinary
Tract Disease   102
   Hematuria   103
   Trauma   104

**Chapter 5: Kidney Failure
and Inflammatory and
Malignant Renal Diseases
and Disorders   105**
Kidney Failure   106
   Acute Failure   106
   Chronic Failure   110
Inflammatory Diseases
Affecting the Kidneys   114
   Bright Disease   114
   Pyelonephritis   118
Other Conditions Affecting the
Kidneys and Renal System   119
   Bartter Syndrome   119
   Cystinuria   122
   De Toni–Fanconi
   Syndrome   122
   Diabetic Nephropathy   123
   Iminoglycinuria   126
   Nephrosclerosis   126
   Nephrotic Syndrome   128
   Renal Cyst   128
   Renal Osteodystrophy   129
   Uremia   130
Malignant Diseases of
the Renal System   131
   Bladder Cancer   132
   Nephroblastoma   136
   Renal Cell Carcinoma   137
   Clear Cell Renal Cell
   Carcinoma   139

**Chapter 6: Evaluation
and Treatment of Renal
Diseases and Disorders**   141
   The Study of Renal Function   141
   Evaluating Renal Function   143
      Quantitative Tests   144
      Renal Biopsy   149
   Evaluation of Urinary
   Function   150
      Uroscopy and Urinalysis   151
      Radiological and Other
      Imaging Investigations   153
   Kidney Transplant   156
      Transplantation and
      Postoperative Care   157
      Data on Kidney Transplant
      Results   159
   Dialysis   160

Conclusion   164

Glossary   165
Bibliography   167
Index   168

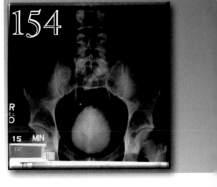

INTRODUCTION

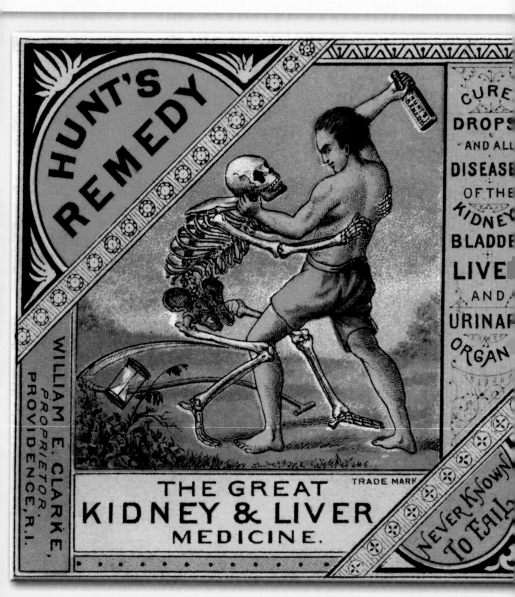

A Victorian advertisement for Hunt's Remedy, which was believed to cure "diseases of the kidneys," among other things. Buyenlarge/Archive Photos/Getty Images

I t is easy to take for granted the complexity of the kidneys and renal system. The intricate network of arteries and nerves, coupled with the unique filtration mechanisms of the kidney, makes understanding the human renal system and treating kidney ailments and dysfunction far from routine. Indeed, the study of the anatomy, physiology, and function of the renal system is an area that has long fascinated scientists, and in this volume readers are taken on a journey through this exquisite organ system.

The human kidneys function to sustain a balance between quantities of water and quantities of electrolytes (salts) in the body. They do this in large part by helping the body conserve water and salts and by facilitating the excretion of waste products. Thus, the kidneys, through regulating the volume and chemical composition of the body's fluids, play a vital role in maintaining a constant internal environment. When concentrations of substances such as sodium, glucose, and wastes cannot be maintained within normal limits, sickness or, in extreme cases, death can occur.

The kidneys, which are bean-shaped and reddish brown in colour, are located in the upper abdominal cavity and are separated from one another by the vertebral column. Aligned vertically, the upper end of each kidney tilts slightly toward the backbone. Along the concave border of each kidney lies a structure known as the hilus, which serves as a gateway for arteries and veins, lymphatic vessels, and nerves running to and from the organ.

About one-fifth of the volume of blood in the human body circulates through the kidneys every minute. Hence, each hour the full volume of blood in the body flows through the kidneys about a dozen times. Each time blood passes through the organs, it is filtered, with the result that wastes are removed and salts and water vital to homeostasis are conserved. Arterial blood is delivered to the kidneys through the renal arteries at maximum pressure and directly from the abdominal aorta. Blood circulation in the kidneys must remain constant so that the organs can continue to monitor water and electrolyte balance uninterrupted. Because of the kidneys' remarkable ability for autoregulation, they can monitor such a balance even if they are cut off from the nervous system. Renal blood flow, however, can be affected by a variety of factors, including fever, physical exertion, pain, and anxiety. Hemorrhaging, asphyxia, and a decline in systematic blood pressure can also affect renal blood flow.

The kidneys contain both sympathetic and parasympathetic nerves (sympathetic nerves, when activated, prepare the body for stress by increasing heart rate and blood flow to muscles and descreasing digestive secretions; parasympathetic nerves, on the other hand, are active when the body is relaxed and increase digestive secretions and reduce heartbeat). Renal nerves carry signals to and from the central nervous system and play an important role in regulating the rate at which blood flows through the kidneys and the pressure the blood exerts against the walls of blood vessels (blood pressure).

The outer region of each kidney is known as the renal cortex. Within the cortex are structures known as nephrons, long tubules that serve as the chief functional units of the kidneys. Each kidney contains approximately one million nephrons. At one end of each nephron is a double-walled cuplike structure called the renal corpuscular capsule, or Bowman's capsule, which houses microscopic blood vessels (capillaries) clustered together, forming what is known as the glomerulus. As blood flows through the glomerulus, fluid is filtered out and passes into the nephron tubule. The filtrate then travels the length of the nephron, and as it progresses along, certain substances are secreted into it and others are reabsorbed from it, thereby altering its composition. Much of the reabsorption of water and sodium chloride from the filtrate occurs along a segment of each nephron called the loop of Henle, which extends into the renal medulla (the inner substance of the kidney). The result of this elaborate filtration process is the production of urine.

Urine produced in the cortex then flows into the kidney's inner tissues. The internal configuration of the kidney can be divided into two main regions: the renal pyramids and the renal pelvis. The former are dark, triangular structures that consist primarily of tubules that transport urine from the cortex to funnel-shaped cavities (calyces) branching from the end of the renal pelvis, where urine is collected before being channeled into the bladder. Hence, the renal pelvis serves as a reservoir for urine, and from it, the urine flows to the urinary bladder via a duct known as the ureter.

The urine produced by the kidney differs markedly in chemical composition from the plasma component of the blood that enters the glomerulus. For example, proteins generally are absent from urine, whereas they are present in blood plasma. This is because most proteins are too large to pass through the filtration membrane in the glomerulus, and thus they remain in the blood. Relative to blood, urine contains high levels of ammonia and a substance called creatinine, which is a breakdown product of the organic acid creatine that is found naturally in muscle. In addition to these substances and water, urine also contains salts, urea (formed from the breakdown of amino acids), and pigmented molecules (formed from the breakdown of blood), which combine to give urine its yellowish colour.

Substances move into or out of the filtrate as it travels through the nephron through different processes. Two types of movement include simple diffusion, in which substances move freely from a region of high concentration to a region of low concentration, and active transport, in which substances are moved across a membrane by an energy-driven mechanism. The different segments of a nephron vary in their permeability to solutes and fluids and rely on different mechanisms of solute and fluid movement. For example, a large percentage of solutes in the filtrate are reabsorbed via active transport from a region of the nephron known as the proximal convoluted tubule. In contrast, the reabsorption of sodium and the movement of potassium and hydrogen ions characterizes the filtration activities that occur in a later section of the nephron known as the distal convoluted tubule. In certain disease states, the tubules may not reabsorb or secrete molecules like they would normally. For example, if blood glucose concentrations are abnormally high, such as in diabetes mellitus, glucose reabsorption from the renal filtrate becomes saturated. The excess glucose remains in the filtrate and is excreted in the urine. The detection of glucose in the urine often is used as a diagnostic measure for diabetes.

The network of blood vessels within each kidney is made up of arteries and arterioles, veins and venules, and a lymphatic network. Many renal arteries branch into offshoots called afferent arterioles that further divide, forming multiple loops of capillaries and carrying blood to the glomeruli in the nephrons. While the arteries and arterioles create a network of pathways carrying blood to different areas of the kidneys, veins and venules (microscopic veins) accompany the arteries and arterioles, draining blood through various pathways. In the renal sinus (the cavity housing the renal pelvis and calyces), veins exiting the kidney fuse to form a single, large renal vein. Running alongside the main renal arteries and veins are lymph channels, which terminate in lymph nodes near the sites of origin of the renal arteries.

The other principal parts of the renal system include the ureters, the urinary bladder, and the urethra. The ureters, as mentioned previously, are narrow ducts that transport urine from the kidneys to the urinary bladder. The wall of each ureter consists of three layers: the outer layer, the muscular layer, and the mucous membrane. Wavelike movements in the ureter muscles propel the passage of urine from the kidney to the bladder.

The urinary bladder is a muscular organ that sits in the front (anterior) region of the pelvic floor and forms in the main urinary reservoir. The bladder has a body with a base, a neck, and an apex. When the bladder is empty, its structure also reveals three different surfaces: one upper surface (the superior surface) and two lower, side surfaces (the inferolateral surfaces). The bladder has its own set of ateries that supply it with blood, and it is innervated by sympathetic and parasympathetic nerve fibres, which facilitate urination. The bladder wall is multilayered and includes a powerful smooth muscle coat, which, when contracted, causes the bladder to empty. The bladder combines certain opposing reflexes to alternately hold urine and initiate urination (micturition) with complete emptying. Whereas the powerful muscle layer ensures emptying upon contraction, there are two muscular sphincters that keep the opening to the urethra closed at all other times. As the bladder fills with urine, it contracts and relaxes. The waves of contraction and relaxation begin at a level that is undetectable but gradually increase in intensity until stimuli reach the brain, causing pain and a sharp rise of pressure.

Voluntary contraction of the muscles in the bladder keeps internal pressure low and prevents urine leakage, but emotional influences such as anxiety can inhibit the bladder's ability to relax upon filling. If the latter arises, involuntary leakage may occur in small quantities.

The urethra is the channel that carries urine from the bladder out of the body. The male urethra is much longer than the female urethra, and it carries semen as well as the secretions of the prostate, bulbourethral, and urethral glands in addition to urine. The urethra wall is comprised of a mucous membrane, submucous layer, and muscular coat, although the muscular coat of the male urethra is incomplete.

Early development of the renal system begins with the pronephros, the most primitive of the three vertebrate kidneys. This often nonfunctional kidney is the first one to develop in the embryo of advanced vertebrates, although it remains active in some primitive fish. In humans, the pronephros is replaced by the mesonephros, which is again replaced by the 10th week of human embryonic development but remains a permanent kidney in amphibians and most fish. After the 10th week of human development, the mesonephros is replaced by the metanephros, a paired organ containing a ureter that leads to the bladder.

The day-to-day volume and composition of urine vary greatly depending on food and fluid intake and fluid loss. The average daily volume or urine is 1.5 litres (about 0.4 gallons) but can rise to three or more litres after heavy intake and fall as low as 500 millilitres (about a pint) after excess sweating. The volume of urine varies throughout the day as well, peaking during the first few hours after awakening and after meals or during the initial period of any exertion. Volume regulation is necessary for maintaining constant plasma osmotic concentration and controlling water content in tissues.

The composition of urine is normally clear, and while pigment breakdown products are responsible for giving urine its usually bright clear yellow colour, vitamins, food dyes, and certain drugs may affect the colour as well and may alter the typical ammonia odour. Likewise, various diseases and disorders affect the overall composition of urine. For example, as in the case of diabetes, the level of a substance normally found in urine (glucose in this example) may be increased. In other instances, a substance not usually found in urine may be detected.

In addition to explaining the anatomy and physiology of the human kidneys and renal system, this volume explores the various diseases that can cause renal dysfunction and kidney failure. It also details the evaluation and treatment of renal diseases and disorders. Quantitative tests, such as the kidney function test, creatinine clearance test, and the insulin clearance test, are tools that doctors and researchers use to further their understanding of normal renal system activity and how to proceed when it fails to function as it should. Although dialysis, transplantation, and postoperative care have become more successful in improving the lives of those suffering from renal disease, the medical community continues to work to understand all the intricacies of an organ system that bears huge responsibility within the human body.

CHAPTER 1

ANATOMY OF THE KIDNEYS AND RENAL SYSTEM

I n many respects the human renal, or urinary, system resembles the renal systems of other mammalian species. However, it has its own unique structural and functional characteristics. Structurally, the human renal system consists of the kidneys, where urine is produced, and the ureters, bladder, and urethra for the passage, storage, and voiding (or elimination from the body) of urine. The eliminatory function of the renal system is often described by the terms *excretory* and *urinary*. The kidneys, however, both secrete and actively retain within the body certain substances that are as critical to survival as those that are eliminated.

The most important functional components of the renal system are the two kidneys, which control the electrolyte (e.g., salt) composition of the blood and eliminate dissolved waste products and excess amounts of other substances from the blood. The latter substances are excreted in the urine, which passes from the kidneys to the bladder by way of two thin muscular tubes called the ureters. The bladder is a sac that holds the urine until it is eliminated through the urethra.

THE KIDNEYS

The human kidneys are reddish brown paired organs and are about 10 cm (about 4 inches) in length. They are

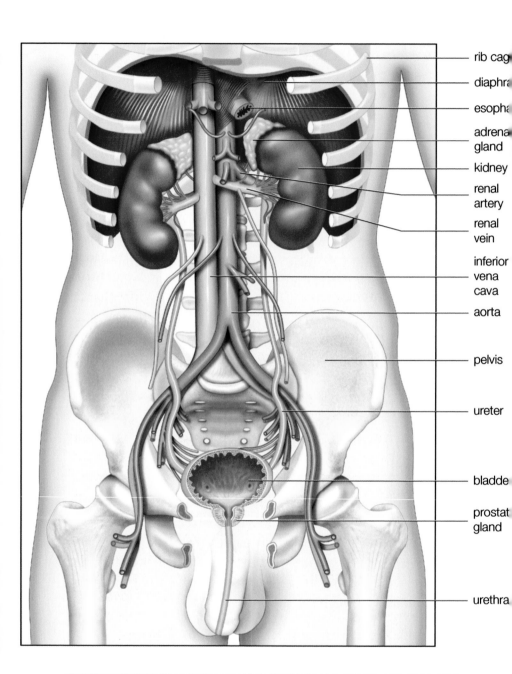

rib cage
diaphragm
esophagus
adrenal gland
kidney
renal artery
renal vein
inferior vena cava
aorta
pelvis
ureter
bladder
prostate gland
urethra

The human kidneys in situ in a male. Encyclopædia Britannica, Inc.

distinguished by their beanlike shape, being concave (curved inward) along the length of one side and convex (curved outward) along the length of the opposite side. Their function is to maintain water balance and to filter metabolic wastes from the blood. (A brief overview of the anatomy of the kidneys is provided here. A detailed discussion can be found in the sections that follow.)

In embryonic development, the kidneys consist of two series of specialized tubules that empty into two collecting ducts, known as the Wolffian ducts. When fully developed, the kidneys contain numerous sophisticated functional units, called nephrons, that filter wastes from the blood and reabsorb water and nutrients. The nephron filtration process results in the final urine product that is ultimately expelled from the body. Each fully developed kidney contains about 1 million to 1.25 million nephrons that filter the entire five-quart water content of the blood every 45 minutes—an equivalent of 160 quarts a day. Of this, only 1½ quarts are excreted. The remainder is reabsorbed by the nephrons.

The kidneys can be divided into two major sections: a somewhat granular outer section called the cortex and a smoother inner section called the medulla. The cortex contains clusters of blood vessels, known as glomeruli, and a series of intricately folded, very fine tubes, known as convoluted tubules. These structures form the upper half of each nephron unit. The lower half of the nephron unit, which consists of the loops of Henle and the collecting tubules, lies in the medulla. The long loops of Henle and the long straight collecting tubules give the tissue of the medulla its smooth, somewhat striated appearance.

The urine that is produced by each nephron passes through the collecting tubule in the medulla and is gathered into a cup-shaped cavity called the renal pelvis. The renal pelvis forms the upper end of the ureter, and the urine gathered there ultimately passes through the ureter to the bladder.

ANATOMICAL LOCATION OF THE KIDNEYS

The kidneys are located high in the abdominal cavity and against its back wall. They are found on either side of the backbone (the vertebral, or spinal, column), between the levels of the 12th thoracic and 3rd lumbar vertebrae, and outside the peritoneum (the membrane that lines the abdomen).

The long axes of the kidneys are aligned with that of the body, but the upper end of each kidney (the pole) is tilted slightly inward toward the vertebral column. Situated in the middle of each kidney on the side facing the vertebral column (the medial concave border) is a deep vertical cleft, called the hilus, which leads to a cavity within the kidney known as the renal (kidney) sinus. The hilus is the point of entry and exit of the renal arteries, veins, lymphatic vessels, and nerves and of the enlarged upper extension of the ureters.

THE RENAL CAPSULE

A thin membranous sheath known as the renal capsule covers the outer surface of each kidney. The capsule is composed of tough fibres, chiefly collagen and elastin (fibrous proteins), that help to support the kidney mass and protect the vital tissue from injury. The number of elastic and smooth muscle fibres found in the capsule tends to increase with the individual's age.

The capsule receives its blood supply ultimately from the interlobar arteries, small vessels that branch off from the main renal arteries. These vessels travel through the cortex of the kidney and terminate in the capsule.

The maximum thickness of the membrane is usually 2–3 mm (0.08–0.12 inch). The capsule surrounds the outer walls and enters into the hollow region of the kidney sinus. The sinus contains the major ducts that transport urine and the arteries and veins that supply the tissue with nutrients and oxygen. The capsule connects to these structures within the sinus and lines the sinus wall.

In a healthy person, the capsule is light reddish-purple in colour, translucent, smooth, and glistening. It can usually be easily stripped from the rest of the kidney's tissue. A diseased kidney frequently sends fibrous connections from the main body of tissue to the capsule, which makes the capsule adhere more strongly.

RENAL VESSELS AND NERVES

The renal arteries arise, one on each side, from a large vessel known as the abdominal aorta. The renal arteries split off from the abdominal aorta at a point a little above the small of the back (opposite the upper border of the second lumbar vertebra). Close to the renal hilus each artery gives off small branches to the adrenal gland and ureter and then further branches into divisions that extend toward the front (anterior) of the renal tissues as well as behind (or posterior to) these tissues. The large veins carrying blood from the kidneys usually lie in front of the corresponding arteries and join the inferior vena cava (a large vein that travels up from the lower region of the body to the right side of the heart) almost at right angles. The left vein is longer than the right vein because the inferior vena cava lies closer to the right kidney.

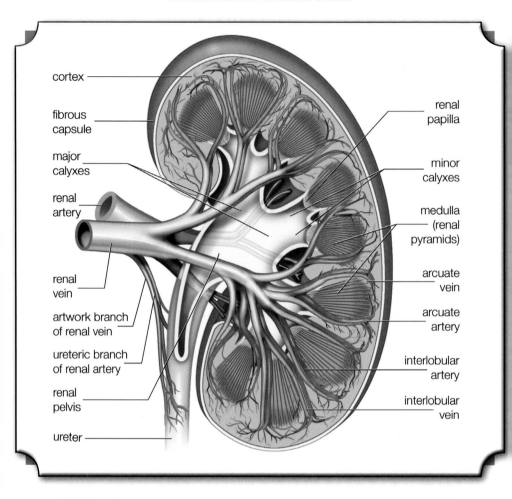

Cross section of the right kidney showing the major blood vessels.
Encyclopædia Britannica, Inc.

The kidneys are supplied with sympathetic and parasympathetic nerves of the autonomic nervous system (the part of the nervous system that controls and regulates internal organs without conscious effort). The renal nerves contain both afferent and efferent fibres (afferent fibres carry nerve impulses to the central nervous system, whereas efferent fibres carry impulses away from the central nervous system).

INTERNAL CONFIGURATION: THE RENAL PYRAMID

The renal pyramids are any of the triangular sections of tissue that constitute the medulla, or inner substance, of the kidney. The pyramids consist mainly of tubules that transport urine from the cortex, or outer, part of the kidney, where urine is produced, to the calyxes, or cup-shaped cavities in which urine collects before it passes through the ureter to the bladder. The renal pyramids are visible in cross sections of kidney tissue as comparatively dark cones in the substance of the renal medulla. The bases of the cones face outward, toward the external surface of the kidney, and the apexes project, either singly or in groups, into the renal sinus.

The point of each pyramid, called the papilla, projects into a small cuplike cavity called a minor calyx. Each kidney has about 12 minor calyxes, which combine to form several major calyxes. The major calyxes then converge into the renal pelvis at the upper end of the ureter. Each group of pyramids that projects into a papilla, together with the portion of cortex that arches over the group, is called a renal lobe.

The surface of the papilla has a sievelike appearance because of the many small openings from which urine droplets pass. Each opening represents a tubule called the duct of Bellini, into which collecting tubules within the pyramid converge. Muscle fibres lead from the calyx to the papilla. As the muscle fibres of the calyx contract, urine flows through the ducts of Bellini into the calyx. The urine then flows to the bladder by way of the renal pelvis and a duct known as the ureter.

Between the pyramids are major arteries known as the interlobar arteries. Each interlobar artery branches over the base of the pyramid. Smaller arteries and capillaries divide off from the interlobar arteries to supply each pyramid and the cortex with a rich network of blood vessels.

7

Blockage of an interlobar artery can cause degeneration of a renal pyramid.

Some animals, such as rats and rabbits, have a kidney composed of only one renal pyramid. In humans each kidney has a dozen or more pyramids.

Internal Configuration: The Renal Pelvis

The renal pelvis is shaped somewhat like a funnel that is curved to one side. It is almost completely enclosed in the deep indentation on the concave side of the kidney, which forms the kidney sinus. The large end of the pelvis contains the cuplike major calyxes that collect urine before it flows on into the urinary bladder.

Like the ureter, the renal pelvis is lined with a moist mucous-membrane layer that is only a few cells thick. The membrane is attached to a thicker coating of smooth muscle fibres, which, in turn, is surrounded by a layer of connective tissue. The mucous membrane of the pelvis is somewhat folded so that there is some room for tissue expansion when urine distends the pelvis. The muscle fibres are arranged in a longitudinal and a circular layer. Contractions of the muscle layers occur in periodic waves known as peristaltic movements. The peristaltic waves help to push urine from the pelvis into the ureter and bladder. The lining of the pelvis and of the ureter is impermeable to the normal substances found in urine. Thus, the walls of these structures do not absorb fluids.

Minute Structure: The Nephron and Loop of Henle

The structural units of the kidneys that actually produce urine are the nephrons. The most primitive

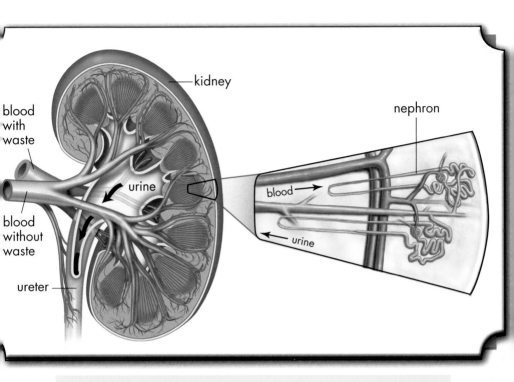

Each kidney has approximately one million nephrons, which filter water and other substances out of the blood to produce urine. Encyclopædia Britannica, Inc.

nephrons are found in the kidneys (pronephros) of primitive fish, amphibian larvae, and embryos of more advanced vertebrates. The nephrons found in the kidneys (mesonephros) of amphibians and most fish, and in the late embryonic development of more advanced vertebrates, are only slightly more advanced in structure. The most advanced nephrons occur in the adult kidneys, or metanephros, of land vertebrates, such as reptiles, birds, and mammals.

Each nephron is a long tubule that is closed, expanded, and folded into a double-walled cuplike structure at one end. This structure, called the renal corpuscular capsule, or Bowman's capsule, encloses a cluster of capillaries (microscopic blood vessels) called the glomerulus. The capsule and glomerulus together constitute a renal corpuscle, also called a malpighian body. Blood flows into and away from the glomerulus through small arteries (arterioles) that enter and exit the glomerulus through the open end of the capsule. This opening is called the vascular pole of the corpuscle.

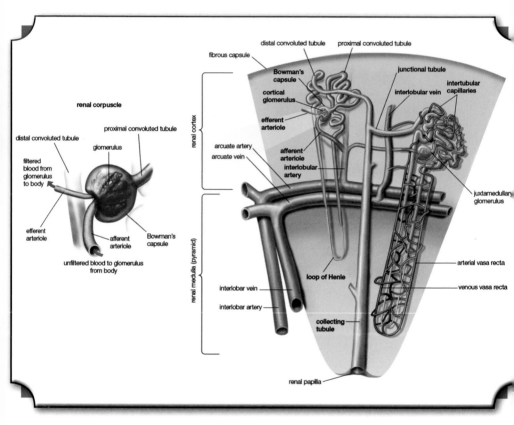

Each nephron of the kidney contains blood vessels and a special tubule. As the filtrate flows through the tubule of the nephron, it becomes increasingly concentrated into urine. Waste products are transferred from the blood into the filtrate, while nutrients are absorbed from the filtrate into the blood. Encyclopædia Britannica, Inc.

The tubules of the nephrons are 30–55 mm (1.2–2.2 inches) long. The corpuscle and the initial portion of each tubule, called the proximal convoluted tubule, lie in the renal cortex. The tubule descends into a renal pyramid, makes a U-shaped turn, and returns to the cortex at a point near its point of entry into the medulla. This section of the tubule, consisting of the two parallel lengths and the bend between them, is called the loop of Henle or the nephronic loop. After its reentrance into the cortex, the tubule returns to the vascular pole (the opening in the cuplike structure of the capsule) of its own nephron. The final portion of the tubule, the distal convoluted tubule, leads from the vascular pole of the corpuscle to a collecting tubule, by way of a short junctional tubule. Several of the collecting tubules join together to form a somewhat wider tubule, which carries the urine to a renal papilla and the renal pelvis.

The principal function of the loop of Henle appears to be the recovery of water and sodium chloride from the urine. This function allows production of urine that is far more concentrated than blood, limiting the amount of water needed as intake for survival. Many species that live in arid environments such as deserts have highly efficient loops of Henle.

The liquid entering the loop is the solution of salt, urea, and other substances passed along by the proximal convoluted tubule, from which most of the dissolved components needed by the body—particularly glucose, amino acids, and sodium bicarbonate—have been reabsorbed into the blood. The first segment of the loop, the descending limb, is permeable to water, and the liquid reaching the bend of the loop is much richer than the blood plasma in salt and urea. As the liquid returns through the ascending limb, sodium chloride diffuses out of the tubule into the surrounding tissue, where its concentration is lower. In the third segment of the loop, the tubule wall can, if necessary, effect further removal of salt, even against the concentration gradient, in an active-transport process requiring the expenditure of energy. In a healthy person the reabsorption of salt from the urine exactly maintains the bodily requirement: during periods of low salt intake, virtually none is allowed to escape in the urine, but, in periods of high salt intake, the excess is excreted.

Although all nephrons in the kidney have the same general disposition, there are regional differences, particularly in the length of the loops of Henle. Glomeruli that lie deep in the renal cortex near the medulla (juxtamedullary glomeruli) possess long loops of Henle that pass deeply into the medulla, whereas more superficial cortical glomeruli have much shorter loops. Among different animal species the length of the loops varies considerably and affects the ability of the species to concentrate urine above the osmotic concentration of plasma (the concentration of dissolved substances in the blood plasma).

The successive sections of the nephron tubule vary in shape and calibre, and these differences, together with differences in the cells that line the sections, are associated with specific functions in the production of urine.

MINUTE STRUCTURE: THE RENAL COLLECTING TUBULES

The primary function of the renal collecting tubules, or ducts of Bellini, is to concentrate and transport urine from the nephrons to larger ducts that connect with the renal calyxes. The collecting tubules connect with the nephron tubules in the cortex.

Each collecting tubule is about 20–22 mm (about 0.8 inch) long and 20–50 micrometres in diameter. The walls of the tubules are composed of cells with hairlike projections, known as flagellae, in the tube's channel. Motions of the flagellae help to move secretions through the tubes. As the collecting tubes become wider in diameter, the cells increase in height so that the wall becomes thicker.

It is thought that the tissue of the kidney's medulla contains a high concentration of sodium. As the collecting tubules travel through the medulla, the concentration of sodium causes water to be extracted through the tubule walls into the medulla. The water diffuses out between the collecting wall cells until the concentration of sodium is equal in the tubes and outside them. Removal of water from the solution in the tubes serves to concentrate the urine content and conserve body water.

Pathologic changes that can afflict the tubules include degeneration or atrophy of the tube walls; deposition of calcium compounds; infection by viruses, bacteria, fungi, or parasites; presence of crystals; dilatation or blockage of the tubes; and malignant tumours.

INTRARENAL NETWORK OF BLOOD VESSELS

The intrarenal network of blood vessels forms part of the blood-processing apparatus of the kidneys. Similar to other organ systems, arteries, veins, and capillaries fulfill vital roles in the function of the kidneys and renal system.

Arteries and Arterioles

The anterior and posterior divisions of each renal artery, mentioned earlier, divide into lobar arteries, each of which enters the kidney substance through or near a renal papilla. Each lobar artery gives off two or three branches, called interlobar arteries, which run outward between adjacent renal pyramids. When these reach the boundary between the cortex and the medulla they split almost at right angles into branches called arcuate arteries that curve along between the cortex and the medulla parallel to the surface of the kidney. Many arteries, called interlobular arteries, branch off from the arcuate arteries and radiate out through the cortex to end in networks of capillaries in the region just inside the capsule. En route they give off short branches called the afferent arterioles, which carry blood to the glomeruli where they divide into four to eight loops of capillaries in each glomerulus.

Near and before the point where the afferent arteriole enters the glomerulus, its lining layer becomes enlarged and contains secretory granules. This composite structure is called the juxtaglomerular apparatus and is believed to be involved in the secretion of renin (an enzyme secreted by the kidney that plays an important role in maintaining blood pressure). The vessels are then reconstituted near the point of entry of the afferent arteriole to become the efferent arterioles carrying blood away from the glomeruli. The afferent arterioles are almost twice as thick as the efferent arterioles because they have thicker muscular coats, but the sizes of their channels are almost the same. Throughout most of the cortex the efferent arterioles redivide into a second set of capillaries, which supply blood to the proximal and distal renal tubules.

The efferent glomerular arterioles of juxtaglomerular glomeruli divide into vessels that supply the contiguous tubules and vessels that enter the bases of the renal pyramids. Known as vasa recta, these vessels run toward the apexes of the pyramids in close contact with the loops of Henle. Like the tubules they make hairpin bends, retrace their path, and empty into arcuate veins that parallel the arcuate arteries.

Normally the blood circulating in the cortex is more abundant than that in the medulla (amounting to over 90 percent of the total), but in certain conditions, such as those associated with severe trauma or blood loss, cortical vessels may become constricted while the juxtamedullary circulation is preserved. Because the cortical glomeruli and tubules are deprived of blood, the flow of urine is diminished and in extreme cases may cease.

Veins and Venules

The renal venules (small veins) and veins accompany the arterioles and arteries and are referred to by similar names. The venules that lie just beneath the renal capsule, called stellate venules because of their radial arrangement, drain into interlobular venules. In turn these combine to form the tributaries of the arcuate, interlobar, and lobar veins. Blood from the renal pyramids passes into vessels, called venae rectae, which join the arcuate veins. In the renal sinus the lobar veins unite to form veins corresponding to the main divisions of the renal arteries, and they normally fuse to constitute a single renal vein in or near the renal hilus.

Lymphatic Network

Lymphatic capillaries form a network just inside the renal capsule and another, deeper network between and around the renal blood vessels. Few lymphatic capillaries appear in the actual renal substance, and those present are evidently associated with the connective tissue framework, while the glomeruli contain no lymphatics.

The lymphatic networks inside the capsule and around the renal blood vessels drain into lymphatic channels accompanying the interlobular and arcuate blood vessels. The main lymph channels run alongside the main renal arteries and veins to end in lymph nodes beside the aorta and near the sites of origin of the renal arteries.

THE URETERS

The ureters are two tubes that transmit urine from each kidney to the bladder. Each tube emerges from each kidney, descends behind the abdominal cavity, and opens into the bladder. At its termination the ureter passes through the bladder wall in such a way that, as the bladder fills with urine, this terminal part of the ureter tends to close.

General Characteristics

Each ureter is about 25–30 cm (9.8–11.8 inches) in length and from 4–5 mm (0.16–0.2 inch) in diameter. Throughout their course they lie behind the peritoneum, the lining of the abdomen and pelvis, and are attached to it by connective tissue.

In both sexes the ureters enter the bladder wall about 5 cm (about 2 inches) apart, although this distance is increased when the bladder is distended with urine. The ureters run obliquely through the muscular wall of the bladder for nearly 2 cm (about 0.8 inch) before opening into the bladder cavity through narrow apertures. This oblique course provides a kind of valvular mechanism. When the bladder becomes distended it presses against the part of each ureter that is in the muscular wall of the bladder, and this helps to prevent the flow of urine back into the ureters from the bladder.

Structure of the Ureteric Wall

The wall of the ureter has three layers, the adventitia (or outer layer), the intermediate, muscular layer, and the lining, made up of mucous membrane. The adventitia consists of fibroelastic connective tissue that merges with the connective tissue behind the peritoneum. The muscular coat is composed of smooth (involuntary) muscle fibres and, in the upper two-thirds of the ureter, has two layers—an inner layer of fibres arranged longitudinally and an outer layer disposed circularly. In the lower third of the ureter an additional longitudinal layer appears on the outside of the vessel. As each ureter extends into the bladder wall its circular fibres disappear, but its longitudinal fibres extend almost as far as the mucous membrane lining the bladder.

The mucous membrane lining increases in thickness from the renal pelvis downward. Thus, in the pelvis and the calyxes of the kidney the lining is two to three cells deep. In the ureter, the lining is four to five cells thick, and in the bladder, it is six to eight cells thick. The mucous membrane of the ureters is arranged in longitudinal folds, permitting considerable dilation of the channel. There are no true glands in the mucous membrane of the ureter or of the renal pelvis. The chief propelling force for the passage of urine from the kidney to the bladder is produced by peristaltic (wavelike) movements in the ureter muscles.

THE URINARY BLADDER

The bladder is the organ for the temporary storage of urine. In humans, it is a greatly expandable muscular sac— in the average adult human, it is uncomfortably distended at a volume of around 350 ml ($\frac{1}{3}$ quart) of urine.

The bladder is connected to the exterior of the body by the urethra. Whereas in females the urethra is separate from the genital tract, in males the ductus, or vas, deferens (sperm-carrying tubes) empty into the urethra, and both urine and semen pass through the urethra to reach the exterior.

Male urinary bladder and urethra

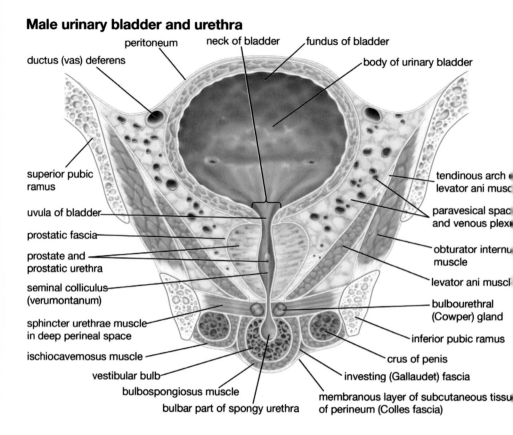

peritoneum   neck of bladder   fundus of bladder
ductus (vas) deferens   body of urinary bladder

superior pubic ramus
uvula of bladder
prostatic fascia
prostate and prostatic urethra
seminal colliculus (verumontanum)
sphincter urethrae muscle in deep perineal space
ischiocavemosus muscle
vestibular bulb
bulbospongiosus muscle
bulbar part of spongy urethra

tendinous arch of levator ani musc
paravesical spac and venous plex
obturator internu muscle
levator ani muscl
bulbourethral (Cowper) gland
inferior pubic ramus
crus of penis
investing (Gallaudet) fascia
membranous layer of subcutaneous tissu of perineum (Colles fascia)

The human male urinary bladder and urethra. Encyclopædia Britannica, Inc.

GENERAL DESCRIPTION

The bladder rests on the anterior part of the pelvic floor, behind the symphysis pubis and below the peritoneum. (The symphysis pubis joins the bodies of the two pubic bones of the pelvis.) The shape and size of the bladder vary according to the amount of urine that the organ contains. When empty it is tetrahedral and lies within the pelvis. When distended it becomes ovoid and expands into the lower abdomen.

The bladder has a body, with a fundus, or base; a neck; an apex; and a superior (upper) and two inferolateral (below and to the side) surfaces, although these features are not clearly evident except when the bladder is empty or only slightly distended. The neck of the bladder is the area immediately surrounding the urethral opening. It is the lowest and most fixed part of the organ. In the male it is firmly attached to the base of the prostate, a gland that encircles the urethra.

The superior surface of the bladder is triangular and is covered with peritoneum. The bladder is supported on the levator ani muscles, which constitute the major part of the floor of the pelvic cavity. The bladder is covered, and to a certain extent supported, by the visceral layer of the pelvic fascia. This fascial layer is a sheet of connective tissue that sheaths the organs, blood vessels, and nerves of the pelvic cavity. The fascia forms, in front and to the side, ligaments, called pubovesical ligaments, that act as a kind of hammock under the inferolateral surfaces and neck of the bladder.

BLOOD AND NERVE SUPPLIES

The blood supply of the bladder is derived from the superior, middle, and inferior vesical (bladder) arteries. The superior vesical artery supplies the dome of the bladder, and one of its branches (in males) gives off the artery to the ductus deferens, a part of the passageway for sperm. The middle vesical artery supplies the base of the bladder. The inferior vesical artery supplies the inferolateral surfaces of the bladder and assists in supplying the base of the bladder, the lower end of the ureter, and other adjacent structures.

The nerves to the urinary bladder belong to the sympathetic and the parasympathetic divisions of the autonomic nervous system. The sympathetic nerve fibres come from the hypogastric plexus of nerves that lie in front of the fifth lumbar vertebra. Sympathetic nerves carry to the central nervous system the sensations associated with distention of the bladder and are believed to be involved in relaxation of the muscular layer of the vesical wall and with contraction of sphincter mechanism that closes the opening into the urethra. The parasympathetic nerves travel to the bladder with pelvic splanchnic nerves from the second through fifth sacral spinal segment. Parasympathetic nerves are concerned with contraction of the muscular walls of the bladder and with relaxation of its sphincter. Consequently they are actively involved in urination and are sometimes referred to as the emptying, or detrusor, nerves.

Structure of the Bladder Wall

The bladder wall has a serous coat over its upper surface. This covering is a continuation of the peritoneum that lines the abdominal cavity. It is called serous because it exudes a slight amount of lubricating fluid called serum. The other layers of the bladder wall are the fascial, muscular, submucous, and mucous coats.

The fascial coat is a layer of connective tissue, such as that which covers muscles. The muscular coat consists of coarse fascicles, or bundles, of smooth (involuntary) muscle fibres arranged in three strata, with fibres of the outer and inner layers running lengthwise, and with fibres of the intermediate layer running circularly. There is considerable intermingling of fibres between the layers. The smooth muscle coat constitutes the powerful detrusor muscle, which causes the bladder to empty.

The circular or intermediate muscular stratum of the vesical wall is thicker than the other layers. Its fibres, although running in a generally circular direction, do interlace. The internal muscular stratum is an indefinite layer of fibres that are mostly directed longitudinally. The submucous coat consists of loose connective tissue containing many elastic fibres. It is absent in the trigone, a triangular area whose angles are at the two openings for the ureters and the single internal urethral opening. Slim bands of muscle run between each ureteric opening and the internal urethral orifice. These are thought to maintain the oblique direction of the ureters during contraction of the bladder. Another bundle of muscle fibres connects the two ureteric openings and produces a slightly downwardly curved fold of mucous membrane between the openings.

The mucous coat, the innermost lining of the bladder, is an elastic layer impervious to urine. Over the trigone it firmly adheres to the muscular coat and is always smooth and pink whether the bladder is contracted or distended. Elsewhere, if the bladder is contracted, the mucous coat has multiple folds and a red, velvety appearance. When the bladder is distended, the folds are obliterated, but the difference in colour between the paler trigonal area and the other areas of the mucous membrane persists. The mucous membrane lining the bladder is continuous with that lining the ureters and the urethra.

THE URETHRA

The urethra is the duct that transmits urine from the bladder to the exterior of the body during urination. The urethra is held closed by the urethral sphincter, a muscular structure that helps keep urine in the bladder until voiding can occur.

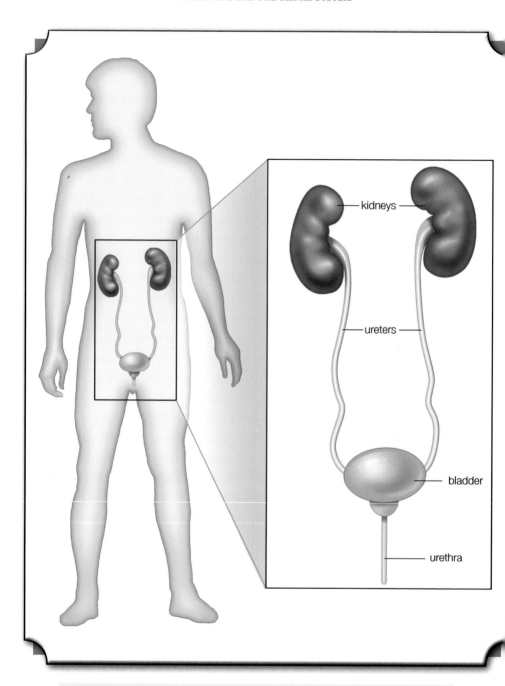

Organs of the renal system. Encyclopædia Britannica, Inc.

Because the urethra is anatomically linked with the reproductive structures in the male, the characteristics of the male's and female's urethra are quite different. The male's urethra is about 20 cm (8 inches) long and passes along the length of the penis before emptying. At its emergence from the bladder, the urethra passes through the prostate gland, and seminal ducts from the testes enter the urethra at each side, making it the pathway for the transmission of semen as well as for the discharge of urine.

The female urethra is embedded within the vaginal wall, and its opening is situated between the labia (the folds of skin that are part of the external female genitalia). The female urethra is much shorter than that of the male, being only 4 cm (about 1.6 inches) long. It opens to the outside just after passing through the urethral sphincter. Both the male and female urethra are subject to bacterial infections.

GENERAL DESCRIPTION

In males, during urination and ejaculation, the urethra opens up, and its diameter then varies from 0.5–0.8 cm (about 0.2–0.3 inch) along its length, but at other times its walls touch and its lining is raised into longitudinal folds. The male urethra has three distinguishable parts, the prostatic, the membranous, and the spongy, each part being named from the structures through which it passes rather than from any inherent characteristics.

The prostatic section of the male urethra commences at the internal urethral orifice and descends almost vertically through the prostate, from the base of the gland to the apex, describing a slight curve with its concavity forward. It is about 2.5–3 cm (1–1.2 inches) long and is spindle-shaped. Its middle portion is the widest and most dilatable part of the urethra. The membranous part of the male urethra is in the area between the two layers of a membrane called the urogenital diaphragm. The urethra is narrower in this area than at any other point except at its external opening and is encircled by a muscle, the sphincter urethrae. The two small bulbourethral glands are on either side of it. The membranous urethra is not firmly attached to the layers of the urogenital diaphragm. The spongy part of the male urethra is that part of the urethra that traverses the penis. It passes through the corpus spongiosum of the penis. The ducts of the bulbourethral glands enter the spongy urethra about 2.5 cm (1 inch) below the lower layer of the urogenital membrane. Except near its outer end, many mucous glands also open into it.

The female urethra is more distensible than the corresponding channel in males and carries only urine and the secretions of mucous glands. It begins at the internal opening of the urethra into the bladder and curves gently downward and forward through the urogenital diaphragm, where it is surrounded, as in the male, by the sphincter urethrae. It lies behind and below the symphysis pubis. Except for its uppermost part, the urethra is embedded in the anterior wall of the vagina. The external urethral orifice is immediately in front of the vaginal opening, about 2.5 cm (1 inch) behind the clitoris.

STRUCTURE OF URETHRAL WALL

The urethra of the male is a tube of mucous membrane supported on a submucous layer and an incomplete muscular coat. The membrane forms longitudinal folds when the tube is empty. These folds are more prominent in the membranous and spongy parts. There are many glands in the mucous membrane, and they are more common in the

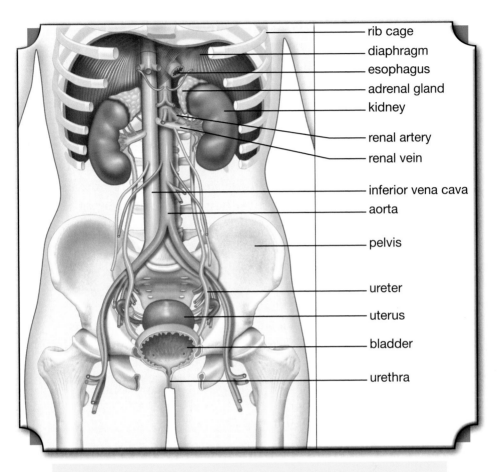

rib cage
diaphragm
esophagus
adrenal gland
kidney

renal artery
renal vein

inferior vena cava
aorta

pelvis

ureter

uterus

bladder

urethra

The kidneys and the female urinary system. Encyclopædia Britannica, Inc.

posterior wall of the spongy part. The submucous layer is composed of fibroelastic connective tissue containing numerous small blood vessels, including more venules than arterioles. The thin muscular coat consists of smooth (involuntary) and striated (voluntary) muscle fibres. The smooth muscular layer, longitudinally disposed, is continuous above with the detrusor muscle of the bladder and extends distally as far as the membranous urethra, where it is replaced and partly surrounded by striated muscle of the external sphincter. The somatic nerves to the external sphincter are the efferent and afferent components of the pudendal nerve, arising from the second, third, and fourth sacral segments of the spinal cord.

The female urethra has mucous, submucous, and muscular coats. As in the male, the lining of the empty channel is raised into longitudinal folds. It also shows mucous glands, mentioned in the preceding paragraphs as existing in the male urethra. The submucous coat resembles that in the male, except that the venules are even more prominent. In both sexes, but especially in females, this layer appears to be a variety of erectile tissue. The muscular coat extends along the entire length of the female urethra and is continuous above with the musculature of the bladder. It consists of inner longitudinal and outer circular layers, and fibres from the latter intermix with those in the anterior wall of the vagina, in which the urethra is embedded.

CHAPTER 2

DEVELOPMENT AND FUNCTION OF THE KIDNEYS AND RENAL SYSTEM

During gestation—the 36–40-week-long period of embryonic and fetal growth between conception and birth—the human kidney progresses through three distinct stages of development. These stages are determined by the development of kidneys that become increasingly complex in structure and function, beginning with the pronephros (or earliest kidney), proceeding to the mesonephros (or intermediate kidney), and culminating in the metanephros (or permanent kidney). Each fully developed metanephros, what is referred to generally by the term *kidney*, carries out the complex filtration process that results in the production of urine.

DEVELOPMENT OF THE RENAL SYSTEM

During embryological development, the tissues of the human kidney arise from the cellular plates called nephrotomes that connect somites (a longitudinal series of blocklike segments of embryonic tissue) with the mesodermal sheets that bound the body cavity. The first kidney to develop in the human embryo is the pronephros. The vestigial pronephros (an evolutionary remnant that is imperfectly developed) is represented solely by several pairs of tubules. These tubules join with separately formed

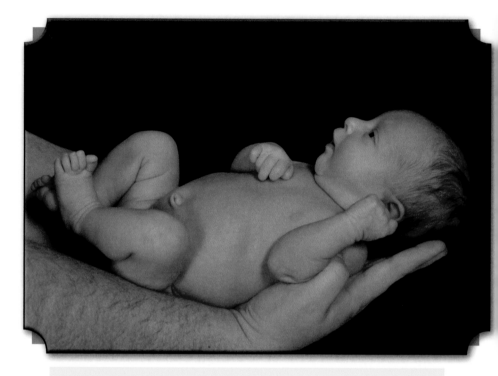

A newborn baby. Shutterstock.com

excretory ducts that grow downward and enter the cloaca, the common outlet for urine, genital products, and intestinal wastes. Frequently nonfunctional, the pronephros is replaced (after 3½ weeks) by the mesonephros.

Some 40 pairs of nephric (kidney) tubules constitute the mesonephros. These tubules join the same excretory ducts as the pronephros. Hereafter these ducts are known as the mesonephric ducts. The two sets of mesonephric tubules serve as functioning kidneys until the 10th week of gestation.

Each permanent kidney, or metanephros, develops still farther tailward. A so-called ureteric primordium buds off each mesonephric duct, near its hind end. The ureteric stem elongates and expands terminally, thereby forming the renal pelvis and calyxes. Continued bushlike branching produces collecting ducts. The early ureteric bud invades a mass of nephrotome tissue. The branching collecting ducts progressively break this tissue up into tiny lumps, each of which becomes a long secretory tubule, or nephron, and joins a nearby terminal twig of the duct system. Continued proliferation of ducts and nephric tissue produces more than 1 million nephrons in each kidney (most adults have about 1 million to 1.25 million nephrons per kidney).

The blind caudal end of the endodermal hindgut absorbs the stem of each mesonephric duct, whereupon the remainder of the duct and the ureter acquire separate openings into the hindgut. This expanded region of the gut, now a potential receptacle for feces, urine, and reproductive products, is known as a cloaca. It next subdivides into a rectum behind and a urogenital sinus in front. The sinus, in turn, will specialize into the urinary bladder and the urethra. The prostate gland develops as multiple buds from the urethra, close to the bladder.

REGULATORY FUNCTIONS OF THE KIDNEYS

The kidney has evolved so as to enable humans to exist on land where water and salts must be conserved, wastes excreted in concentrated form, and the blood and the tissue fluids strictly regulated as to volume, chemical composition, and osmotic pressure. Under the drive of arterial pressure, water and salts are filtered from the blood through the capillaries of the glomerulus into the lumen, or passageway, of the nephron, and then most of the water and the substances that are essential to the body are reabsorbed into the blood. The remaining filtrate is drained off as urine. The kidneys, thus, help maintain a constant internal environment despite a wide range of changes in the external environment.

The kidneys regulate three essential and interrelated properties of the tissues—water content, acid-base balance, and osmotic pressure—in such a way as to maintain electrolyte and water equilibrium. In other words, the kidneys are able to maintain a balance between quantities of water and the quantities of such chemicals as calcium, potassium, sodium, phosphorus, and sulfate in solution. Unless the concentrations of mineral ions such as sodium, crystalloids such as glucose, and wastes such as urea are maintained within narrow normal limits, bodily malfunction rapidly develops leading to sickness or death.

The removal of both kidneys causes urinary constituents to accumulate in the blood (uremia), resulting in death in 14–21 days if untreated. (The term *uremia* does not mean that urea is itself a toxic compound responsible for illness and death.) Whenever the blood contains an abnormal constituent in solution or an excess of normal constituents including water and salts, the kidneys excrete these until normal composition is restored. The kidneys are the only means for eliminating the wastes that are the end products of protein metabolism. They do not themselves modify the waste products that they excrete, but transfer them to the urine in the form in which they are produced in other parts of the body. The only exception to this is their ability to manufacture ammonia. The kidneys also eliminate drugs and toxic agents. Thus, the kidneys eliminate the unwanted end products of metabolism, such as urea, while limiting the loss of valuable substances, such as glucose. In maintaining the acid-base equilibrium, the kidneys remove the excess of hydrogen ions produced from the normally acid-forming diet and manufacture ammonia to remove these ions in the urine as ammonium salts.

Vigorous sweating during heavy activity. Mike Ehrmann/Getty Images

To carry on its functions the kidney is endowed with a relatively huge blood supply. The blood processed in the kidneys amounts to some 1,200 ml a minute, or 1,800 litres (about 475 gallons) a day, which is 400 times the total blood volume and roughly one-fourth the volume pumped each day by the heart. Every 24 hours 170 litres (45 gallons) of water are filtered from the bloodstream into the renal tubules. By far the greater part of this—some 168.5 litres (44.5 gallons) of water together with salts dissolved in it— is reabsorbed by the cells lining the tubules and returned to the blood. The total glomerular filtrate in 24 hours is no less than 50–60 times the volume of blood plasma (the blood minus its cells) in the entire body. In a 24-hour period, an average man eliminates only 1.5 litres (0.4 gallons) of water, containing the waste products of metabolism, but the actual volume varies with fluid intake and occupational and environmental factors. With vigorous sweating it may fall to 500 ml (about a pint) a day. With a large water intake it may rise to three litres (0.8 gallons), or six times as much. The kidney can vary its reabsorption of water to compensate for changes in plasma volume resulting from dehydration or overhydration.

The kidneys also perform certain nonexcretory functions. They secrete substances that enter the blood. These are of three kinds: renin, which is concerned indirectly with the control of electrolyte balance and blood pressure; erythropoietin, which is important for the formation of hemoglobin and red blood cells, especially in response to anemia or deficiency of oxygen reaching the body tissues; and 1,25-dihydroxycholecalciferol, which is the metabolically active form of vitamin D. Finally, although the kidneys are subject to both nervous and humoral (hormonal) control, they do possess a considerable degree of autonomy. For example, function continues in an organ isolated from the nervous system but kept alive with circulating fluid. Indeed, if this were not so kidney transplantation would be impossible.

RENAL BLOOD CIRCULATION

The circulation of blood within the kidneys and renal tissues occurs through a complex, self-regulating network of vessels. In fact, regardless of systemic blood flow (with the exception of extreme changes in systemic blood pressure), the renal circulatory system is capable of maintaining a steady rate of blood flow and a steady glomerular blood pressure. This enables the kidneys to sustain an optimal rate of filtration and reabsorption, which is vital to overall physiological homeostasis. Although the precise mechanisms mediating the regulatory capacity of renal circulation are unclear, this ability appears to be a function of a combination of factors, including the anatomical arrangement of renal blood vessels, muscles, and nerve fibres and the existence of an internal autoregulatory system.

INTRARENAL BLOOD PRESSURES

The renal arteries are short and spring directly from the abdominal aorta, so that arterial blood is delivered to the kidneys at maximum available pressure. As in other vascular beds, renal perfusion is determined by the renal arterial blood pressure and vascular resistance to blood flow. Evidence indicates that in the kidneys the greater part of the total resistance occurs in the glomerular arterioles. The muscular coats of the arterioles are well supplied with sympathetic vasoconstrictor fibres (nerve fibres that induce narrowing of the blood vessels), and there is also a small parasympathetic supply from the vagus and splanchnic nerves that induces dilation of the vessels. Sympathetic stimulation causes vasoconstriction and reduces urinary output. The vessel walls are also sensitive to circulating epinephrine and norepinephrine hormones, small amounts of which constrict the efferent arterioles and large amounts of which constrict all the vessels, and to angiotensin, which is a constrictor agent closely related to renin. Prostaglandins may also have a role.

FACTORS THAT AFFECT RENAL FLOW

The kidney is able to regulate its internal circulation regardless of the systemic blood pressure, provided that the latter is not extremely high or extremely low. The forces that are involved in maintaining a circulation of the blood in the kidneys must remain constant if the monitoring of the water and electrolyte composition of the blood is to proceed undisturbed. This regulation is preserved even in the kidney cut off from the nervous system and, to a lesser extent, in an organ removed from the body and kept viable by having salt solutions of physiologically suitable concentrations circulated through it. In the body, this process is commonly referred to as autoregulation.

The exact mechanism by which the kidney regulates its own circulation is not known, but various theories have been proposed: (1) Smooth muscle cells in the arterioles may have an intrinsic basal tone (normal degree of contraction) when not affected by nervous or humoral (hormonal) stimuli. The tone responds to alterations in perfusion pressure in such a way that when the pressure falls the degree of contraction is reduced, preglomerular resistance is lowered, and blood flow is preserved. Conversely, when perfusion pressure rises, the degree of contraction is increased and blood flow remains constant. (2) If the renal blood flow rises, more sodium is present in the fluid in the distal tubules because the filtration rate increases. This rise in the sodium level stimulates the secretion of renin from the juxtaglomerular apparatus with the formation of angiotensin, causing the arterioles to constrict and blood flow to be reduced. (3) If systemic blood pressure rises, the renal blood flow remains constant because of the increased viscosity of the blood. Normally, the interlobular arteries have an axial (central) stream of red blood cells with an outer layer of plasma so that the afferent arterioles skim off more plasma than cells. If the arteriolar blood pressure rises, the skimming effect increases, and the more densely packed axial flow of cells in the vessels offers increasing resistance to the pressure, which has to overcome this heightened viscosity. Thus, the overall renal blood flow changes little. Up to a point, similar considerations in reverse apply to the effects of reduced systemic pressure. (4) Changes in the arterial pressure modify the pressure exerted by the interstitial (tissue) fluid of the kidney on capillaries and veins so that increased pressure raises, and decreased pressure lowers, resistance to blood flow.

The renal blood flow is greater when a person is lying down than when standing, and it is higher in fever. It is reduced by prolonged vigorous exertion, pain, anxiety, and other emotions that constrict the arterioles and divert blood to other organs. It is also reduced by hemorrhage and asphyxia and by depletion of water and salts, which is severe in shock, including operative shock. A large fall in systemic blood pressure, as after severe hemorrhage, may so reduce renal blood flow that no urine at all is formed for a time. In this instance, death may occur from suppression of glomerular function. Simple fainting causes vasoconstriction and reduced urine output. Urinary secretion is also stopped by obstruction of the ureter when back pressure reaches a critical point.

GLOMERULAR PRESSURE

The importance of these various vascular factors lies in the fact that the basic process occurring in the glomerulus is one of filtration, the energy for which is furnished by the blood pressure within the glomerular capillaries. Glomerular pressure is a function of the systemic pressure as modified by the tone (state of constriction or dilation) of the afferent and efferent arterioles, as these open or close spontaneously or in response to nervous or hormonal control.

In normal circumstances glomerular pressure is believed to be about 45 millimetres of mercury (mmHg), which is a higher pressure than that found in capillaries elsewhere in the body. As is the case in renal blood flow, the glomerular filtration rate is also kept within the limits between which autoregulation of blood flow operates. Outside these limits, however, major changes in blood flow occur. Thus, severe constriction of the afferent vessels reduces blood flow, glomerular pressure, and filtration rate, while efferent constriction causes reduced blood flow but increases glomerular pressure and filtration.

THE ROLE OF HORMONES IN RENAL FUNCTION

Certain hormones and hormonelike substances are intimately related to renal function. Some of these, such as vasopressin (or antidiuretic hormone), are produced outside the kidney and travel to the kidney via the blood as chemical messengers. Others are produced within the kidney and appear to exert only a local effect. Vasopressin regulates water excretion by increasing the permeability of the collecting ducts to water and salt and by accelerating water and ion transfer in a direction determined by the osmotic gradient. The receptors at the base of the brain form part of the feedback mechanism that (1) stimulates vasopressin output if the osmotic concentration of extracellular fluid (ECF) is high, so as to concentrate the urine, and (2) reduces vasopressin output and so dilutes the urine if osmotic concentration of ECF and of plasma falls.

The hormones of the adrenal cortex are also important in influencing renal function, directly or indirectly. In stress situations, as after an injury or a surgical operation, the output of hydrocortisone and other corticosteroids is increased because the adrenals are stimulated by adrenocorticotropin (or adrenocorticotropic hormone, ACTH), a secretion of the pituitary gland. Hydrocortisone increases protein breakdown, and consequently the output of nitrogen in the urine, and affects water metabolism. Lack of hydrocortisone reduces the power of the kidney to deal with normal water loads. The hormone also promotes sodium retention and loss of potassium and hydrogen ions by the kidney.

Aldosterone influences electrolyte metabolism by facilitating the reabsorption of sodium ions at the distal tubules, also at the expense of hydrogen and potassium excretion. The action of aldosterone has been described as priming the sodium reabsorption pump. It is the adrenal hormone most important to tubular function. It also influences the ability of the bowel to absorb sodium, and thus its level of production profoundly influences overall sodium balance. Deficiency of aldosterone allows a steady loss of sodium in the urine, causing a fall in blood pressure that may result in fainting.

The action of the parathyroid glands, which are endocrine glands located close to and behind the thyroid gland in the lower neck, is to increase blood calcium by mobilizing calcium from the bones and other sources. If this hormone functions to excess, as in tumours of the glands, the urinary loss of calcium is much increased and calcium stones tend to form in the kidneys and the bladder. Parathyroid hormone also increases the renal excretion of phosphate and accelerates the conversion of hydroxylated vitamin D to the dehydroxylated form in the kidney. The pituitary growth hormone facilitates protein synthesis and decreases the urinary loss of nitrogen. The sex hormones estrogen and progesterone exert an ill-defined activity as regards salt and water metabolism.

Among the prostaglandins, a group of hormonelike fatty acids synthesized throughout the body, the ones found in the kidney tissues appear to exert local influence on various aspects of renal function. Unlike true hormones, prostaglandins are not transported away from their site of origin by the blood. The interstitial and collecting duct cells of the kidney produce a characteristic prostaglandin, PGE_2, and the renal cortex produces PGI_2, or prostacyclin. Renal prostaglandins interact with the renin–angiotensin system in several ways. The renal cortex prostaglandin PGI_2 mediates the increased release of renin in response to decreases in renal blood flow. The angiotensin subsequently formed in the plasma stimulates production of the interstitial and duct cell prostaglandin (PGF_2), which itself inhibits angiotensin-induced vasoconstriction. For this reason the renal cortex prostaglandin is thought to be an important vasodilator, maintaining renal blood flow when this is threatened (for example, after blood loss). Prostaglandins may also inhibit the action of vasopressin on the distal tubule and collecting ducts, and the interstitial and duct cell prostaglandin may have a direct effect in inhibiting renal tubular sodium reabsorption. However, the relative importance of these different actions in the healthy human is not known.

Another substance that causes the dilation of blood vessels, the enzyme kallikrein, may also exert an influence on renal blood flow. Kallikrein is secreted by renal tubules and is added to the urine in the distal tubules. It activates the conversion of kininogen to bradykinin, which is also a powerful vasodilator. Bradykinin is inactivated by a kininase, which also converts angiotensin I to angiotensin II, a substance that causes the constriction of blood vessels. Thus the same enzyme that inactivates the vasodilator bradykinin catalyzes the production of the vasoconstrictor angiotensin II. This relationship again suggests a delicately balanced internal control system.

Dopamine is a putative renal hormone that may affect salt balance. The sympathetic nerves that travel to the kidney, the terminals of which release catecholamines such as norepinephrine, are not believed to be important in controlling tubular salt reabsorption. Transplanted human kidneys function adequately despite the lack of any nerve supply and so renal nerves are not essential.

However, because dopamine (also a catecholamine released at sympathetic nerve endings) is present in urine in amounts far in excess of the amount that might be filtered from the blood, it may be deduced that some dopamine is formed within the kidney. It is now believed that dopamine is formed enzymatically within the kidney from its precursor, l-dopa, which freely circulates in the blood, and that only small amounts are released by sympathetic nerve endings. Dopamine is a powerful natriuretic substance (i.e., one capable of increasing urinary salt loss) and renal vasodilator. Its role in salt balance, renal function, and blood pressure control remains speculative.

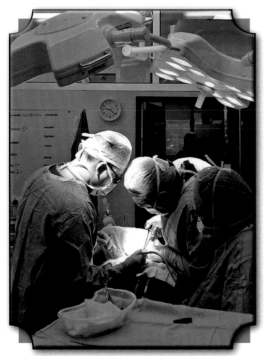

Surgeons at Birmingham Hospital conducting a kidney transplant. Christopher Furlong/Getty Images

The most recently identified hormone that influences renal function is secreted by special "stretch receptor" cells in the atria of the heart in response to a rise in atrial pressure, as during heart failure. This hormone, called atrial natriuretic peptide (ANP), exerts a vasodilator effect on the kidney and also reduces tubular reabsorption of sodium. Both actions result in increased urinary elimination of salt and water and tend to restore atrial pressure toward the normal. It is probably an important hormone controlling the volume of the extracellular fluid.

Of special significance to the hormonal regulation of renal function is the renin-angiotensin system, a physiological system that regulates blood pressure. Renin is an enzyme secreted into the blood from specialized cells that encircle the arterioles at the entrance to the glomeruli of the kidneys. The renin-secreting cells, which compose the juxtaglomerular apparatus, are sensitive to changes in blood flow and blood pressure. The primary stimulus for increased renin secretion is decreased blood flow to the kidneys, which may be caused by loss of sodium and water (as a result of diarrhea, persistent vomiting, or excessive perspiration) or by narrowing of a renal artery.

Renin catalyzes the conversion of a plasma protein called angiotensinogen into a decapeptide (consisting of 10 amino acids) called angiotensin I. An enzyme in the serum called angiotensin-converting enzyme (ACE) then converts angiotensin I into an octapeptide (consisting of eight amino acids) called angiotensin II. Angiotensin II acts via receptors in the adrenal glands to stimulate the secretion of substances called catecholamines and of aldosterone, which stimulates salt and water reabsorption by the kidneys, and the constriction of small arteries (arterioles), which causes an increase in blood pressure. Angiotensin II further constricts blood vessels through its inhibitory actions on the reuptake into nerve terminals of the hormone norepinephrine.

Drugs that inhibit ACE, and thus block the conversion of angiotensin I to angiotensin II, are used to lower blood pressure in patients with hypertension. Blood pressure also can be lowered using drugs that are designed to block the receptors to which angiotensin II must bind to exert its actions.

BIOLOGICAL CONSIDERATIONS

The rate of renal blood flow and the rate of filtration by the nephrons are also influenced by a number of physiological processes. For example, in women, during most of the pregnancy period the glomerular filtration rate (the average rate at which substances are filtered out of the plasma) is increased by as much as 50 percent, corresponding to an increase in renal blood flow of up to 25 percent in the middle three months of pregnancy. Glycosuria is frequent and is caused by increased glucose loading of the filtrate. There is some sodium retention with a tendency to abnormal accumulation of serous fluid (edema), and some protein may appear in the urine. Anatomical changes include enlargement and dilation of the pelvis and ureters, caused by both hormonal action and partial ureteric obstruction by the gravid uterus. These changes may be responsible for the increased susceptibility to urinary tract infection during pregnancy.

The kidneys of the fetus begin to function well before birth, as indicated by a steady rise in the urea and uric acid content of the amniotic fluid in which the fetus exists. The fetus probably swallows fluid and voids it as urine. But even at birth, half the work of excretion is still being carried out via the placental circulation and the maternal kidneys, and this dependence is abruptly curtailed. Kidney function is far from fully developed in the newborn infant. The glomerular filtration rate is only some 30 ml (1 ounce) per minute per square metre of body surface, compared to 75 (2.5 ounces) in the adult, and tubular function does not attain adult performance until the end of the first year. The 24-hour output of urine is only some 20 ml. The output of water and the renal clearance of sodium, potassium, and phosphate is low, and the urine is dilute and often

A night shift worker. The inversion of natural sleep cycles causes a shift in electrolyte and water output by the renal system. Peter Macdiarmid/Getty Images

contains protein. Because the kidney has such a poor capacity to excrete solids, the infant is exposed to the dehydrating effect of vomiting and diarrhea, which readily induce renal failure.

There is an increased urine output at the commencement of muscular exercise, due to the general stimulation of circulation, but a later falling off with the fatigue and sweating caused by severe prolonged exertion. The 24-hour rhythm in output has been mentioned. The small output in the early morning hours is a practical convenience to prevent disturbance of sleep.

If the natural sleep rhythm is inverted, as by working on night shift, electrolyte and water output follow suit. The urine is acidic at night and becomes less so, or alkaline, on rising. Output is maximal during the first waking hours and rises after meals. Because of all this variation in water and solute output, any analytic study of urine components must be conducted on specimens obtained over a 24-hour period.

CHAPTER 3

THE PHYSIOLOGY OF URINARY EXCRETION

The physiology of urinary excretion is in large part represented by the involved metabolic processes carried out by the kidneys. Despite the superficial complexity of urine production and excretion, at its most fundamental level, the physiology of these processes centres on basic mechanisms that govern the movement of substances across cellular membranes. Among these mechanisms are osmosis, the movement of molecules down their concentration gradient (from a region of high concentration to a region of low concentration), and active transport, the movement of molecules against their concentration gradient (from a region of low concentration to a region of high concentration). The combined effect of such processes is the filtration of wastes from the blood with the balance between water and solutes, such as sodium and chloride, in the blood maintained.

Urine formation and excretion are influenced by multiple factors. For example, environmental factors directly affect the volume and composition of normal urine, which vary widely between individuals and from one day to the next. Such variation in healthy persons occurs primarily as a result of fluctuations in fluid intake and fluid loss.

PRINCIPAL FEATURES OF URINE AND ITS EXCRETION

Urine is the liquid solution of metabolic wastes and certain other, often toxic, substances that the renal organs withdraw from the circulatory fluids and expel from the body.

The composition of urine tends to mirror water needs. For example, freshwater animals usually excrete very dilute urine. Marine animals tend to combat water loss to their salty environment by excreting concentrated urine. Some marine species develop methods actively to expel salts. Terrestrial animals, depending on their habitat, usually retain water and secrete a highly concentrated urine.

In humans, the formation of urine begins in the nephrons of the kidneys by filtration of blood plasma into the nephron. The fluid found within the nephron is essentially the same as blood plasma without the macromolecules (e.g., proteins). As the fluid passes along the nephron tube, water and useful plasma components such as amino acids, glucose, and other nutrients are reabsorbed into the bloodstream, leaving a concentrated solution of waste material called final, or bladder, urine. It consists of water, urea (from amino acid metabolism), inorganic salts, creatinine, ammonia, and pigmented products of blood breakdown, one of which (urochrome) gives urine its typically yellowish colour. In addition, any unusual substances for which there is no mechanism of reabsorption into the blood remain in the urine. The products of nucleic acid breakdown are present as uric acid in humans.

Urination, or micturition, is the process of excreting urine from the urinary bladder. Nerve centres for the control of urination are located in the spinal cord, the brainstem, and the cerebral cortex (the outer substance of the large upper portion of the brain). Both involuntary and voluntary muscles are involved.

The major contractile muscle of the bladder is the detrusor. Urination involves either sustained contractions or short intermittent contractions of the detrusor along with contraction of the muscles in the urethra, the duct from the urinary bladder that conducts urine from the body.

In humans and most other animals, voiding of the bladder is influenced by the volume of urine it contains. When 100–150 ml (3.4–5 ounces) of urine accumulate, the first sensations of a need to void are felt. The feeling increases in intensity as more urine accumulates, and it becomes uncomfortable at a bladder volume of 350–400 ml (11.8–13.5 ounces). Impulses from the pelvic nerves mediate the sensations of bladder filling, painful distension, and the conscious need to urinate.

A slowly filling bladder adapts progressively to the pressure from increased volume. Hence, a bladder that is rapidly filled stimulates urination faster than one that fills slowly. When enough pressure is sensed by the walls of the bladder, the detrusor muscle contracts, the bladder neck and opening to the urethra relax, and the contents of the bladder are emptied. Normally the bladder empties completely.

Voluntary restraint of urination involves inhibition of bladder contraction, closure of the opening to the urethra, and contraction of the abdominal muscles. The ability to start and stop the flow of urine depends largely on the normal functioning of the muscles of the pelvic floor, the abdominal wall, and the diaphragm (the muscular partition between the abdomen and the chest). Infants' lack of inhibitory control over urination is related to the immaturity of the nervous system.

Likewise, degeneration or destruction of certain areas of the central nervous system leads to incontinence due to the so-called neurogenic bladder. Such incontinence may be a dribbling overflow from a permanently distended bladder, or an efflux (outflow) from a contracted bladder whose outlet is always open.

If the full bladder is not emptied, it becomes overdistended. In time, bladder distension can cause bleeding, ulcerations, and rupture of the bladder wall. Obstruction to the outflow of urine can follow enlargement of the

Infants require diapers because of their lack of control over urination.
Rayes/Lifesize/Thinkstock

prostate (the gland in males that encircles the urethra close to the bladder), swelling of the urethral tissue around its channel, fibrous stricture of the urethra, or contraction of the muscles at the openings of the bladder and the urethra. Usually urine is retained until the pressure in the bladder overcomes the obstruction. With moderately chronic retention and stress, the detrusor muscle increases in tone and the contractile force of the bladder is increased. When overdistension occurs over long periods, the detrusor muscle produces small rhythmic contractions that cause dribbling of urine. With continued distension, the muscle can become paralyzed, and urine voiding takes place only by overflow. This condition is known as passive incontinence. There may also be flow of urine back to the kidneys under these conditions, causing failure of kidney function.

FORMATION AND COMPOSITION OF URINE

RELATIVE COMPOSITION OF PLASMA AND URINE IN NORMAL MEN		
	PLASMA g/100 ML	URINE g/100 ML	CONCENTRATION IN URINE
water	90–93	95	—
protein	7–8.5	—	—
urea	0.03	2	×60
uric acid	0.002	0.03	×15
glucose	0.1	—	—
creatinine	0.001	0.1	×100
sodium	0.32	0.6	×2
potassium	0.02	0.15	×7
calcium	0.01	0.015	×1.5
magnesium	0.0025	0.01	×4
chloride	0.37	0.6	×2
phosphate	0.003	0.12	×40
sulfate	0.003	0.18	×60
ammonia	0.0001	0.05	×500

The urine leaving the kidneys differs considerably in composition from the plasma that enters the kidneys. The study of renal function must account for these differences. Examples of such differences include the absence of protein and glucose from the urine, a change in the pH of urine as compared with that of plasma, and the high levels of ammonia and creatinine in the urine, while sodium and calcium remain at similar low levels in both urine and plasma.

A large volume of ultrafiltrate (i.e., a liquid from which the blood cells and the blood proteins have been filtered out) is produced by the glomerulus into the capsule. As this liquid traverses the proximal convoluted tubule, most of its water and salts are reabsorbed, some of the solutes completely and others partially—in other words, there is a separation of substances that must be retained from those due for rejection. Subsequently the loop of Henle, distal convoluted tubule, and collecting ducts are mainly concerned with the concentration of urine to provide fine control of water and electrolyte balance.

GLOMERULAR FILTRATION

Urine formation begins as a process of ultrafiltration of a large volume of blood plasma from the glomerular capillaries into the capsular space, colloids such as proteins being held back while crystalloids (substances in true solution) pass through. In humans, the average capillary diameter is 5 to 10 micrometres (a micrometre is 0.001 mm, or 3.9×10^{-5} inch). The wall of each loop of capillaries has three layers. The inner layer consists of flat nucleated endothelial cells arranged to form numerous pores, or fenestrae, 50–100 nanometres in diameter (a nanometre is 0.000001 mm, or 3.9×10^{-8} inch), which allow the blood to make direct contact with the second layer, a basement membrane. The basement membrane of the capillaries, similar to that which occurs in the lining of many other structures and organs, is a continuous layer of hydrated collagen and glycopeptides. Although once thought to be homogeneous, it appears to consist of three layers that differ in the content of polyanionic glycopeptides. The membrane is negatively charged (anionic), owing to its relatively high content of sialic and aspartic acids. Also

49

present are glycosaminoglycans, such as heparin sulfate. The third, external layer consists of large epithelial cells called podocytes. These cells make contact with the outer surface of the basement membrane by slender cytoplasmic extensions called pedicels (foot processes). These processes are slightly expanded at their point of contact with the basement membrane and are separated from each other by slitlike spaces about 20 to 30 nanometres across. A fine membrane (slit diaphragm) closes the slitlike spaces near the basement membrane.

There are two physical processes by which glomerular filtrate may pass the barrier of the glomerular wall—simple diffusion and bulk flow. In bulk flow, the solute in the glomerular filtrate with water passes through pores in the basement membrane. In either case the ultimate restriction to the passage of filtrate appears to lie in the hydrated gel structure of the basement membrane. The negative electrostatic charge in the membrane is an additional restrictive force for negatively charged anionic macromolecules, such as albumin (molecular weight 69,000), while larger protein molecules are restricted by size alone. On the other hand, proteins of smaller molecular size, such as neutral gelatin (molecular weight 35,000), pass through freely. It is possible that the endothelial cell layer may also help to exclude very large molecules and blood cells and that a similar effect is exerted by the slit pores and diaphragm.

The normal process of glomerular filtration depends upon the integrity of the glomerulus, which in turn depends upon its proper nutrition and oxygenation. If glomeruli are damaged through disease or lack of oxygen they become more permeable, allowing plasma proteins to enter the urine. Special cells that may be concerned with the formation and maintenance of the basement membrane of the glomerular walls are called mesangial cells. These lie between loops of the glomerular capillaries and form a stalk or scaffolding for the capillary network. They are themselves embedded in a matrix of glycosaminoglycan similar to that of the glomerular capillary basement membrane and may be responsible for its formation. The mesangial cells are also responsible for ridding the basement membrane of large foreign molecules that may be held there in the course of certain diseases. These cells proliferate and the mesangial matrix enlarges in the course of immunologically induced diseases affecting the glomerulus.

TUBULE FUNCTION

EFFECT OF TUBULAR REABSORPTION ON URINE (ILLUSTRATIVE 24-HOUR FIGURES)		
	GLOMERULAR FILTRATE	URINE	TUBULAR REABSORPTION (PERCENT)
water	170 l	1.5	99.1
glucose	170 g	—	100
sodium	560 g	5 g	99.1
chloride	620 g	9 g	98.5
phosphate	5.1 g	1.2 g	76.5
calcium	17 g	0.2 g	98.8
urea	51 g	30 g	41.4
sulfate	3.4 g	2.7 g	20.6

The role of the tubules may be assessed by comparing the amounts of various substances in the filtrate and in the urine. It is apparent that the filtrate must be modified in the tubules to account for the differing compositions of filtrate and final urine. For example, modifications must be made to allow for the total absence of glucose in the final urine, the much smaller volume of urine than filtrate, or for the acidity of urine compared with the neutrality of the filtrate.

As the filtrate passes along the proximal tubule, most of its water and salts are reabsorbed into the blood of the network of capillaries around the tubules. Of other substances, some are reabsorbed completely, others in part, because this portion of the nephron separates substances that must be retained in the body from those destined for excretion in the urine. The function of the proximal tubule is essentially reabsorption of filtrate in accordance with the needs of homeostasis (equilibrium), whereas the distal part of the nephron and collecting duct are mainly concerned with the detailed regulation of water, electrolyte, and hydrogen-ion balance. All of these processes occur in the tubules through both chemical and physical means, and all are subject to hormonal regulation. Although the urine normally differs markedly from filtrate, if tubule function is progressively reduced in experimental situations by cooling or poisoning, the urine will come increasingly to resemble the filtrate. Also, the more rapidly filtration occurs, the less time there is for the urine to be modified during its passage through the tubules.

REABSORPTION FROM THE PROXIMAL TUBULE

Reabsorption affects all the glucose of the filtrate, up to 70 percent of its water and sodium (the remainder is absorbed in the distal tubule), most of the potassium and chloride ions, some of the uric acid, 40 percent of the urea, and little or none of the sulfate. Of the total solids 75 percent are reabsorbed in the proximal tubule. The first part of the tubule absorbs amino acids, glucose, lactate, and phosphate. The whole convolution absorbs sodium, potassium, calcium, and chloride and, by removing bicarbonate, acidifies the fluid slightly.

The tubule has only a certain capacity for reabsorption. Thus, normally all the glucose arriving in the filtrate is absorbed. But if plasma glucose is increased to high enough levels, the glucose arrives at the tubule cells faster than it can be absorbed—a condition that occurs in diabetes. In other words, there is a critical rate of delivery determined by plasma concentration and filtration rate, and a maximum reabsorptive capacity for each substance in the filtrate. The rate of tubular reabsorption has an upper maximum value that is constant for any given substance. Consequently, if the plasma level rises sufficiently, all surplus of the substance will pass out in the urine. This is true even for glucose, which is totally reabsorbed under normal conditions. On the other hand, the upper maximum value is much lower for phosphate, so there is normally always some phosphate in the urine. The proximal tubular reabsorption of phosphate is also affected by the phosphate content of the filtrate and is influenced by parathyroid hormone. Phosphate competes with glucose for reabsorption, and its reabsorption is reduced by parathyroid hormone and by vitamin D and is increased, at least for some time, by a high dietary phosphate intake.

The amino acids also have their own maximum tubular reabsorption values, but these are high enough to ensure that they are entirely reabsorbed under normal conditions. In certain rare inherited disorders such as cystinuria, in which there is excessive excretion of cystine, their reabsorption is reduced.

Vitamin D3 capsules. Shutterstock.com

The reabsorption of about 70 percent of the sodium ions in the filtrate means that a similar value of water in the filtrate must accompany these ions as a vehicle to prevent a rising osmotic gradient (i.e., to prevent a rising difference in the concentration of the sodium solution inside and outside the tubule). The energy required for the reabsorption of sodium into the blood uses 80 percent of the oxygen consumed by the kidney and represents one-eighth of the oxygen consumption of a person at rest. There is no evidence for active water transport, and the large volume of water reabsorption occurs passively in response to the movement of sodium. Since sodium is quantitatively the major osmotically active solute, the overall effect is to keep the fluid that remains in the tubular lumen, though much reduced in volume, roughly isosmotic with the original glomerular filtrate.

The active reabsorption of sodium (a positively charged ion) into the blood leaves the fluid remaining in the proximal tubule electronegative with respect to the peritubular fluids (fluids that are adjacent to or surrounding the tubule). This provides a driving force for the reabsorptive transport of negatively charged ions such as chloride, bicarbonate, and organic solutes. Reabsorption of neutral molecules such as urea into the blood is also driven by active sodium transport. Because the tubular epithelium is less permeable to urea and creatinine than it is to water or chloride, however, the free passive movement of water out of the tubular lumen leads to a rising luminal concentration of urea (i.e., above the concentration in the original filtrate with plasma). As a result, a smaller proportion of filtered urea or creatinine than of sodium or water is reabsorbed into the blood, resulting in the elimination of a considerable amount in the urine.

REABSORPTION FROM THE LOOP OF HENLE

About one-third of the volume of the glomerular filtrate enters the descending limb of the loop of Henle. This fluid is isosmotic with plasma, meaning that it has the same osmotic pressure as plasma. The reabsorptive characteristics of the descending thin limb and those of the bend of the loop differ greatly from those of the ascending thick limb. The thin epithelium lining the thin limb is permeable to water and solute and has no power of active transport. Accordingly, the fluid entering the limb and the bend of the loop acquires the concentration of the fluid of the surrounding interstitial peritubular fluid. In contrast, the thick ascending limb lined by taller cells has low permeability to water and to urea but actively transports sodium and chloride into the peritubular fluid around both limbs. As a result this fluid in the medullary and deep cortical regions of the kidney becomes highly concentrated, reaching concentrations of up to four times that of the plasma (1,200 mosmoles per litre), mainly owing to the accumulation of sodium and chloride. This accumulation of solute, essential to the formation of a concentrated urine, is discussed in further detail in the following sections.

REABSORPTION FROM THE DISTAL CONVOLUTED TUBULE

The active transport of sodium out of the ascending limb renders the fluid entering the distal convoluted tubule less concentrated than plasma. Active sodium reabsorption continues throughout the whole of the distal tubule, and this extends to the early part of the collecting duct. As this part of the nephron is relatively impermeable to water, a large concentration gradient of sodium and chloride between the luminal fluid and the plasma is maintained, the concentration of sodium in the tubule being kept well below that of the plasma. The luminal fluid here is also markedly electronegative to the surrounding tissues. The mechanism of sodium reabsorption appears to be directly linked to the secretion of potassium and of hydrogen ions into the tubule from the blood and is greatly influenced by the hormone aldosterone, which is secreted by the adrenal gland when the body's sodium level is deficient.

THE CONCENTRATION OF URINE

As already indicated, the loop of Henle is critical to the ability of the kidney to concentrate urine. The high concentration of salt in the medullary fluid (the fluid between the cells in the medulla tissue) is believed to be achieved in the loop by a process known as countercurrent exchange multiplication. The principle of this process is analogous to the physical principle applied in the conduction of hot exhaust gases past cold incoming gas so as to warm it and conserve heat. That exchange is a passive one. But in the kidney the countercurrent multiplier system uses energy to "pump" sodium and chloride out of the ascending limb of the loop into the medullary fluid. From there it enters (by diffusion) the filtrate (isotonic with plasma—having the same salt concentration as plasma) that is entering the descending limb from the proximal tubule, thus raising its concentration a little above that of plasma. As this luminal fluid in turn reaches the ascending limb, and subsequently the distal tubule, it in turn provides more sodium to be pumped out into the surrounding fluid or blood, if necessary, and transported (by diffusion) back into the descending limb. This concentrating process continues until the osmotic pressure of the fluid is sufficient to balance the resorptive power of the collecting ducts in the

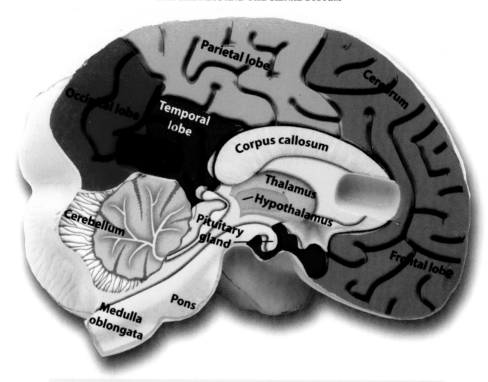

A model of the brain highlighting the hypothalamus at the centre. Shutterstock.com

medulla, through which all of the final urine must pass. This resorptive capacity in the ducts is regulated by vasopressin which is secreted by the hypothalamus and stored in the posterior pituitary gland at the base of the brain.

In the presence of vasopressin the medullary collecting ducts become freely permeable to solute and water. As a consequence the fluid entering the ducts (en route to the renal pelvis and subsequent elimination) acquires the concentration of the interstitial fluid of the medulla, and hence the urine becomes concentrated. On the other hand in the absence of vasopressin the collecting ducts are impermeable to solute and water. Thus, the fluid in the lumen, from which some solute has been removed, remains less concentrated than plasma, and the urine is dilute.

The secretion of vasopressin by the hypothalamus and its release from the posterior pituitary is part of a feedback mechanism responsive to the tonicity of plasma (tonicity is the sum of the concentrations of the solutes that exert an osmotic pressure).

This interrelation between plasma osmotic pressure and vasopressin output is mediated by specific and sensitive receptors at the base of the brain. These receptors are particularly sensitive to sodium and chloride ions. At normal blood tonicity there is a steady receptor discharge and a steady secretion of vasopressin. If the plasma becomes hypertonic (i.e., has a greater osmotic pressure than normal), either from the ingestion of salt, or from shortage of water, receptor discharge increases, triggering increased vasopressin output, and more water leaves the collecting ducts to be absorbed into the blood. If the osmotic pressure of plasma becomes low, the reverse is the case. Thus water ingestion dilutes body fluids and reduces or stops vasopressin secretion. The urine becomes hypotonic, and the extra water is excreted in the urine.

The situation is complex because there are also receptors sensitive to changes in blood volume that reflexively inhibit vasopressin output if there is any tendency to excessive blood volume. Exercise increases vasopressin output and reduces urinary flow. The same result may follow emotional disturbance, fainting, pain, and injury, or the use of certain drugs such as morphine or nicotine. Diuresis is an increased flow of urine produced as the result of increased fluid intake, absence of hormonal activity, or the taking of certain drugs that reduce sodium and water reabsorption from the tubules. If vasopressin secretion is inhibited by the drinking of excess water, or by disease or the presence of a tumour affecting the base of the brain, water diuresis results. In this case, the rate of urine formation will approach the rate of 16 ml (.54 ounces) per minute filtered at the glomeruli. In certain disorders of the pituitary in which vasopressin secretion is diminished or absent—e.g., diabetes insipidus—there may be a fixed and irreversible output of a large quantity of dilute urine.

TUBULAR SECRETION

The only difference between secretory and reabsorptive tubular mechanisms lies in the direction of transport. Secretory mechanisms involve the addition of substances to the filtrate from the plasma in the peritubular capillaries. The small amount of secretion that does occur, except for the secretion of potassium and uric acid, takes place in the proximal tubule. Hydrogen ions are also secreted and ammonia is generated, but they are special cases. As in the case of reabsorption, secretion occurs both passively and actively against an electrochemical gradient.

Several drugs are actively secreted, and some of these appear to share a common pathway so that they may compete with each other for a limited amount of energy. This may be turned to therapeutic advantage in the case of penicillin, which is eliminated partly by tubular secretion. The drug probenecid, which can be given simultaneously, competes with penicillin at its secretory site and thus helps to raise the level of penicillin in the blood in the treatment of certain infections. Endogenous (originating within the body) compounds that are secreted also include prostaglandins, bile salts, and hippurate. Uric acid derived from nucleoproteins freely passes the glomerular barrier and is normally largely reabsorbed in the proximal tubule. In some circumstances, however, it is also secreted by other parts of the same convoluted tubule.

The secretion of potassium by the distal tubule is one of the most important events in the kidney as its control is fundamental to the maintenance of overall potassium balance. More than 75 percent of the filtered potassium is reabsorbed in the proximal tubule and in the ascending limb of the loop of Henle, and this percentage remains virtually constant, irrespective of how much is filtered. The amount eliminated in the urine, which is ultimately determined by the dietary intake, is controlled by the distal convoluted tubule. In persons consuming a normal diet, probably about 50 percent of the urinary potassium is secreted into the urine by the distal tubules. This amount can be adjusted according to body need. One of the several factors that influence potassium secretion is a hormone secreted by the cortex of the adrenal gland, aldosterone. In the absence of aldosterone and other mineralocorticoids (adrenocortical steroids affecting electrolyte and fluid balance), potassium secretion is impaired, and potentially dangerous amounts can accumulate in the blood. Excess aldosterone promotes potassium excretion.

REGULATION OF ACID-BASE BALANCE

The cells of the body derive energy from oxidative processes that produce acidic waste products. Acids are substances that ionize to yield free protons, or hydrogen ions. Those hydrogen ions that derive from nonvolatile acids—such as lactic, pyruvic, sulfuric, and phosphoric acids—are eliminated in the urine. The kidney contains transport mechanisms that are capable of raising the concentration of hydrogen ions in the urine to 2,500 times that in the plasma or, when appropriate, lowering it to one-quarter that of the plasma.

Theoretically, acidification of urine could be brought about either by the secretion of hydrogen ions into the tubular fluid or by the selective absorption of a buffer base (a substance capable of accepting hydrogen ions; e.g., filtered bicarbonate). Evidence indicates that both filtration and secretion are essential to hydrogen ion excretion and that both proximal and distal convoluted tubules are involved.

The bulk of the bicarbonate filtered at the glomerulus is reabsorbed in the proximal tubule, from which it passes back into the peritubular capillaries. This mechanism is designed to keep the normal plasma bicarbonate concentration constant at about 25 millimoles per litre. When the plasma concentration falls below this level, no bicarbonate is excreted and all filtered bicarbonate is reabsorbed into the blood. This level is often referred to as the bicarbonate threshold. When the plasma bicarbonate rises above 27 millimoles per litre, bicarbonate appears in the urine in increasing amounts.

The brush borders of the cells of the proximal tubules are rich in the enzyme carbonic anhydrase. This enzyme facilitates the formation of carbonic acid (H_2CO_3) from CO_2 and H_2O, which then ionizes to hydrogen ions (H^+) and bicarbonate ions (HCO_3^-). The starting point for bicarbonate reabsorption is probably the active secretion of hydrogen ions into the tubular fluid. These ions may be formed under the influence of carbonic anhydrase from CO_2 liberated from oxidation of cell nutrients and H_2O already in the cells. The filtered base, bicarbonate, accepts the hydrogen ions to form carbonic acid, which is unstable and dissociates to form CO_2 and H_2O. The partial pressure of CO_2 in the filtrate rises, and, as CO_2 is highly diffusible, it passes readily from the tubular fluid into the tubular cells and the blood, and the water is either dealt with in the same way or is excreted. In the meantime the proximal tubular cells are actively reabsorbing filtered sodium, which is balanced by the HCO_3^- formed within the cells from the CO_2 generated by the hydrogen ions in the luminal fluid. Thus the bicarbonate actually reabsorbed is not that which was originally the filtrate, but the net effect is the same as if this were the case.

Other bases besides HCO_3^- may buffer the hydrogen ions secreted into the distal tubules. In addition, the ions may combine with ammonia also secreted by the tubules. The most important nonbicarbonate base present in the filtrate is dibasic phosphate (Na_2HPO_4), which accepts hydrogen ions to form monobasic phosphate (NaH_2PO_4). A measure of the amount of hydrogen ion in the urine that is buffered by bases such as bicarbonate and phosphate is made by the titration of urine with strong base until the pH of the plasma from which the filtrate is derived (7.4) is achieved. This is called the titratable acidity of urine and usually amounts to between 20 and 40 millimoles of H^+ per day.

In normal circumstances about two-thirds of the hydrogen ions to be secreted in the urine is in the form of ammonium salts (e.g., ammonium chloride). Ammonia (NH_3) is not present in plasma or filtrate but is generated in the distal tubular cells and passes into the lumen probably by passive diffusion down a concentration gradient. In the lumen the NH_3 combines with hydrogen ions secreted into the tubule to form ammonium ions (NH_4^+), which are then trapped in the lumen because the lipid walls of the tubular cells are much less permeable to the charged than to the uncharged molecules.

It is now known that ammonia is formed from the hydrolysis of glutamine (an amino acid) to form glutamic acid and ammonia by the enzyme glutaminase. A further molecule of ammonia is obtained by the deamination of glutamic acid to form glutaric acid, which is then metabolized. The more acidic the urine is, the greater is its content of ammonium ions. The introduction of hydrogen ions (e.g., from the diet) stimulates production of ammonium by the tubular cells. The ammonium is excreted in the urine as ammonium salts of surplus anions (negative ions) such as chloride, sulfate, and phosphate, thus sparing for retention other cations (positive ions) such as sodium or potassium.

In summary, hydrogen ion secretion can be considered in three phases. The first occurs in the proximal tubule, where the net result is tubular reabsorption of filtered bicarbonate. The second and third phases take place in the distal tubule, where monobasic phosphate and ammonium salts are formed. The total tubular cell secretion of hydrogen ion is therefore the sum of titratable acidity, the amount of ammonium ion excreted, and the amount of bicarbonate ion reabsorbed. The last may be assessed by calculating the amount of bicarbonate filtered (i.e., plasma concentration of bicarbonate × glomerular filtration rate and subtracting any bicarbonate excreted in the urine). Total hydrogen ion secretion normally amounts to 50–100 millimoles per day but may rise considerably above this in disorders associated with excess acid production, such as diabetes.

VOLUME AND COMPOSITION OF URINE

The volume and composition of normal urine vary widely from day to day, even in healthy individuals, as a result of food and fluid intake and of fluid loss through other channels as affected by environmental conditions and exercise. The daily volume averages 1.5 litres (about 1.6 quarts) with a range of 1–2.5 litres (1.05–2.6 quarts), but after copious sweating it may fall as low as 500 ml (16.9 ounces), and after excess fluid intake it may reach three litres (3.2 quarts) or more. There is also variation within a 24-hour period. Excretion is reduced in the early hours, maximal during the first few hours after rising, with peaks after meals and during the early stages of exertion. The urine produced between morning and evening is two to four times the night volume. The excessive secretion of urine (polyuria) of chronic renal disease is typically nocturnal.

The volume of urine is regulated to keep plasma osmotic concentration constant, to control the total water content of the tissues, and to provide a vehicle for the daily excretion to the exterior of some 50 grams (1 gram = 0.035 ounces) of solids, mostly urea and sodium chloride. In a man who ingests 100 grams of protein and 10 grams of salt daily, the urine will contain 30 grams of urea and 10 grams of salt. There are many other possible constituents, but they amount to less than 10 grams overall.

SOME URINE CONSTITUENTS (g/24 HOURS)	
urea	25–30
uric acid	0.6–0.7
creatinine	1.0–1.2
hippuric acid	0.7
ammonia	0.7
amino acids	3
sodium	1–5 (NaCl 15.0)
potassium	2–4
calcium	0.2–0.3
magnesium	0.1
chloride	7
phosphate	1.7–2.5
sulfate	1.8–2.5

Some urinary constituents—the products of metabolism of nitrogenous substances obtained from food—vary widely in relation to the composition of the diet. Thus the excretion of urea and sulfate is dependent on the diet-protein content. A high-protein diet may yield a 24-hour output of 17 grams of nitrogen, a low-protein diet of the same calorific value only three to four grams.

The urine is normally clear. It may be turbid from calcium phosphate, which clears if acetic acid is added. Microscopic deposits include occasional casts, vaguely resembling in form the renal tubules from whose lining they have been shed. An ammoniacal smell is the result of decomposition of urea to ammonia by bacteria and is commonly present on babies' diapers. Certain foods and drugs may cause distinctive odours. The colour of urine depends on its concentration but is normally a bright clear yellow from the pigment urochrome, an end product of protein metabolism. There are also traces of other pigments: urobilin and uroerythrin. The colour may be influenced as well by vitamins, food dyes, beetroot, and certain drugs.

The specific gravity of urine may vary between 1.001 and 1.04 but is usually 1.01–1.025. Such variation is normal, and a fixed low specific gravity is an indication of chronic renal disease. If fluid intake is stopped for 24 hours, a normal kidney will secrete urine with a specific gravity of at least 1.025. There is a limit to the concentrating powers of the kidney, so that the urine is rarely more than four times as concentrated as plasma. In order to excrete their normal solute load, the kidneys need a minimum water output of 850 ml (28.7 ounces) as a vehicle. This volume is often called the minimum obligatory volume of urine. If this is not available from intake it has to be withdrawn from the tissues, causing dehydration. But the usual intake is well above the minimum and the

Urine samples. Shutterstock.com

urine is rarely at its maximum possible concentration. The reaction of the urine is usually acid, with an overall range of pH 4 to 8 (lemon pie has a pH of 2.3; the value 8 is slightly alkaline, about equal to the pH of a 1 percent solution of sodium bicarbonate).

Foreign proteins of molecular weight less than 68,000 are excreted in the urine, while those of the plasma are retained in the body. If, however, the kidneys are damaged by disease or toxins, the glomeruli will transmit some of the normal serum albumin and globulin and the urine will coagulate on warming. Normally, the urine contains only very small amounts of protein (less than 50 mg, or 0.002 ounces, per 24 hours). However, protein content in the urine is increased after exercise, in pregnancy, and in some persons when standing (orthostatic albuminuria). The protein loss may be greatly increased in certain chronic renal diseases. In nephrotic syndrome, for example, it may even reach 50 grams in a 24-hour period. Certain specific and easily identifiable proteins appear in the urine in diseases associated with the overgrowth of cells that make immunoglobulins.

Glucose is found in the urine in diabetes mellitus. In some healthy persons, however, there may also be an abnormal amount of glucose in the urine because of a low threshold for tubular reabsorption, without any disturbance of glucose metabolism. Lactosuria (abnormal amount of lactose in the urine) may occur in nursing mothers. Ketone bodies (acetone, acetoacetic acid) are present in traces in normal urine but in quantity in severe untreated diabetes and in relative or actual carbohydrate starvation (e.g., in a person on a high-fat diet).

The urine may contain hemoglobin or its derivatives after hemolysis (liberation of hemoglobin from red blood cells), after incompatible blood transfusion, and in malignant malaria (blackwater fever). Fresh blood may derive from bleeding in the urinary tract. Bile salts and pigments are increased in jaundice, particularly the obstructive variety. Urobilin is greatly increased in certain diseases such as cirrhosis of the liver.

Porphyrins are normally present only in minute amounts but may be increased in erythropoietic porphyria, in which cells in the bone marrow overproduce porphyrins relative to hemoglobin synthesis. The presence of porphyrins also may increase after ingestion of sulfonamides and some other drugs.

The normally small quantities of amino acids in the urine may be much increased in advanced liver disease, in failure of tubular reabsorption, and in certain diseases due to inborn errors of protein metabolism. Phenylketonuria, a disease identified by the presence of phenylpyruvic acid in the urine, is due to lack of the enzyme phenylalanine hydroxylase, so that phenylalanine is converted not to tyrosine but to phenylpyruvic acid. The presence of this acid in blood and tissues causes intellectual disability. The condition may be readily detected if the urine of every newborn infant is tested. Restriction of phenylalanine in the diet in such cases may be beneficial. Alkaptonuria, a disease identified by the presence of homogentisic acid in the urine, is due to lack of the enzyme that catalyzes the oxidation of homogentisic acid. Deposits of the acid in the tissues may cause chronic arthritis or spinal disease. Other such disorders are cystinuria, the presence of the amino acid cystine in the urine, when the bladder may contain cystine stones, and maple syrup urine disease, another disorder involving abnormal levels of amino acid in the urine and blood plasma.

URINE COLLECTION AND EMISSION

From the nephrons the urine enters the final 15 or 20 collecting tubules that open on to each papilla of the renal medulla, projecting into a minor calyx. These open into two or three major calyxes, and these in turn open into the renal pelvis, which connects with the upper expanded portion of the ureter.

Urine is passed down the channel of the renal pelvis and ureter by a succession of peristaltic waves of contraction that begin in the muscle fibres of the minor calyxes, travel out to the major calyxes and then along the ureter every 10–15 seconds. Each wave sends urine through the ureteric orifice into the bladder in discontinuous spurts. These can be seen through a cystoscope if a dye is injected into the bloodstream. Gravity aids this downward flow, which is faster when one is standing erect. Though the overall picture suggests that there is a pacemaker (a set of specialized cells capable of rhythmic contractions) near the pelviureteric junction, this has never been satisfactorily demonstrated in the tissue. The pressure in the renal pelvis is normally low, but the smooth muscle coat of the ureter is a powerful one and the pressure above an obstructed ureter may rise as high as 50 mm (1.9 inches) of mercury. The ureters are doubly innervated from the splanchnic nerves above and the hypogastric network below.

THE BLADDER

The bladder is a hollow organ of variable capacity with a powerful intermediate muscle coat that empties the organ when it contracts and two muscular sphincters that keep the exit closed at all other times. This smooth muscle coat constitutes the powerful detrusor muscle. At the base of the bladder the region of the bladder neck, or trigone, is demarcated by the two ureteric orifices and the internal opening of the urethra. Muscle fibres loop around the urethral opening to form the internal sphincter, which is under involuntary control. The external sphincter consists of two layers of striated muscles under voluntary control.

The mucous membrane lining the bladder is distensible. It is ridged in the empty organ and smoothed out in distension. In micturition the longitudinal muscle of the bladder shortens to widen the bladder neck and allow urine to enter the urethra. The urethra normally contains no urine except during the act of micturition, its walls remaining apposed by muscle tone. The external sphincter can maintain continence even if the internal sphincter is not functioning.

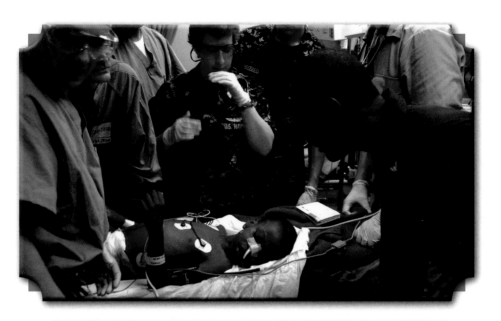

A child with a bladder injury. U. S. Navy photo by MC3c Timothy Wilson

The innervation of the bladder and urethra is complex and important. Essentially, there are three groups of nerves: (1) The parasympathetic nerves constitute the main motor supply to the detrusor. These nerves stimulate contraction of the detrusor, raise pressure within the bladder, relax the internal sphincter, and cause emptying. Afferent parasympathetic channels convey impulses from stretch receptors in the bladder wall to higher centres, permitting cognizance of the state of distension of the organ and stimulating the desire to micturate. (2) The sympathetic nerves stimulate closure of the ureteric and internal urethral orifices and contraction of the internal sphincter, and their action on the detrusor is inhibitory. The effect is to prevent bladder outflow. Thus the sympathetic nerves act to control the situation in the distending bladder up to the point when evacuation can be deferred no longer. Afferent paths in the sympathetic system convey sensations of pain, overdistension, and temperature from the mucosa of the bladder and the urethra. (3) The somatic nerves cause contraction of the external sphincter. Their sensory fibres relay information as to the state of distension of the posterior urethra.

Both the parasympathetic nerves and the somatic nerves (pudendal nerve) to the external sphincter relay impulses to the second through fourth sacral segments of the spinal cord, which constitute a reflex centre for the control of bladder function. This centre connects with higher centres in the brain by ascending and descending fibres in the spinal cord.

BLADDER FUNCTION IN URINATION

Certain reflexes combine to ensure both maintenance of a steady holding state for urine and normal progressive micturition with complete emptying. When the internal pressure of the bladder rises, it contracts. It also contracts when urine enters the urethra.

Both bladder sphincters are normally closed. As the organ fills with urine, the contractile response of the muscle wall causes a rise in internal pressure. Relaxation then occurs as an active process of adjustment so that the organ may hold its contents at a lower pressure. As urine continues to enter the bladder, this rise and fall of pressure continues in steplike fashion, with the final pressure always gradually rising.

The repeated transient contraction waves at first are small and are not consciously felt. Later, stimuli reach the brain and cause pain and a sharp rise of pressure. These later major contractions can be inhibited voluntarily. The desire to micturate begins at around a content of 400 ml (13.5 ounces), but it can be voluntarily overridden until the content reaches 600–800 ml (20.3–27 ounces), with a resulting pressure within the bladder of up to 100 mm (3.9 inches) of water. Until this point the sphincters remain contracted to keep the urethral exit closed, but eventually the desire to micturate becomes urgent and irrepressible. Until that time, voluntary inhibition of the detrusor and contraction of the perineal muscles have kept the internal pressure as low as possible and have prevented urine leakage. The threshold is dependent to some extent on the rate of filling and is higher when filling is slow. Training affects the amount the bladder can retain. In young children the situation is less controllable, and even small amounts of urine may excite reflex evacuation. Emotional influences are important. Anxiety inhibits the capacity of the bladder to relax on filling, so that under conditions of stress there may be some involuntary passage of small quantities of urine.

Neural Control of Urination

Micturition is a complex activity, partly reflex and unconscious and mediated by the lower spinal cord centres, and partly under conscious control by the higher centres of the brain. Voluntary micturition begins with willed messages from the brain that reach the bladder via the motor fibres of the pelvic nerves to stimulate the detrusor, at the same time actively relaxing both urethral sphincters. But the reflexes already mentioned ensure that, once the process has begun and urine has entered the urethra, the contraction of the detrusor will continue and the sphincters will remain relaxed until evacuation is complete and the bladder empty. Evacuation is aided by voluntary contraction of a wide range of accessory muscles. The muscles of the abdominal wall contract to increase pressure on the bladder from without. The diaphragm descends and the breath is held. At the same time there is relaxation of the muscles of the perineal floor. Thus voluntary initiation and control of micturition is effected partly by an active process of stimulating parasympathetic sacral nerve outflow, partly by removing the normal inhibition exerted by the higher centres on the reflex centres in the spinal cord. Once begun, micturition is carried through to completion by lower and higher centres acting in concert. Sensory messages from the urine-distended urethra also play a part. It follows that even if a bladder is not particularly distended and if reflex emptying is not urgent, the bladder can nevertheless be evacuated by voluntary contraction of the abdominal wall, so initiating the reflex process that, once begun, takes over.

CHAPTER 4

RENAL DISORDERS OF FLUID REGULATION AND URINARY FUNCTION

A variety of disorders—from infections and inflammations to tumours to disorders of hormone regulation—can compromise the function of the renal system. The two primary renal functions affected by disease include the elimination of wastes and the conservation of an appropriate amount and quality of body fluid. Indeed, many of the manifestations of renal disease can be accounted for in terms of disturbance of these two functions, and the alleviation of symptoms in those renal diseases that cannot be cured depends on knowledge of how these two functions are affected.

The mechanism of urinary excretion can be altered by structural changes in the lower urinary tract, by infection, or by neurological disorders that lead to abnormal emptying of the bladder. Disturbance of the lower urinary tract is an important cause of pain and distress, notably during pregnancy and in the elderly, and it can lead to serious and progressive damage to the kidneys, either by interfering with the drainage of urine or by allowing bacterial infection to have access to the kidney.

EFFECTS OF ABNORMAL RENAL FUNCTION ON BODY FLUID

Renal disease in its diverse forms can lead to bodily deficits or excesses of water, sodium, potassium, and magnesium, and also to protein deficits occasioned by great losses of protein in the urine. Inability of the kidney to function normally may lead to retention in the blood of the waste products of protein metabolism, such as urea and uric acid, and of other nitrogenous compounds such as creatinine. There may be abnormally high levels of phosphates in the blood, which in turn can lead to low blood levels of calcium. The calcium deficiency can cause tetany, a condition marked by muscular spasms and pain, and calcium may be lost from the bones in the process of restoring normal calcium levels in the blood and tissue fluid. For descriptive purposes, changes in volume, changes in composition, and protein depletion of renal origin will be discussed separately, but these disturbances can and often do coexist.

Though body fluid is most readily apparent in the bloodstream, it is present, and in larger amounts, in the tissues, both between the cells (interstitial fluid) and within them (intracellular fluid). Extracellular fluids, which include interstitial fluid and blood plasma, amount to 25 percent of body weight and contain sodium as their predominant cation (positive ion; metals and hydrogen in solution are cations). Intracellular fluids, amounting to 33 percent of body weight, have potassium as their predominant cation. These various "compartments" of body fluid are in osmotic equilibrium, so that if solute (e.g., sodium chloride) is added to the extracellular compartment so as to increase the concentration of the extracellular solution, water will join it to reduce the concentration, and that compartment will increase. An increase in extracellular fluid, if it is considerable, may be clinically apparent as edema, a swelling of the tissues by fluid, which can usually be displaced by firm pressure. Edema is present in acute inflammation of the kidney (nephritis), in protein deficiency of renal origin, and in chronic nephritis complicated by heart failure associated with abnormally high blood pressure. A factor common to all these states is failure of the kidneys to excrete sodium and water in adequate amounts.

The kidneys in such edematous states need not themselves be diseased. For example, normal kidneys, in a patient with heart failure, may retain sodium when handicapped in their function by poor circulation and by abnormal amounts of sodium-retaining hormones, such as aldosterone. Increase in extracellular fluids is the only volume change that is both common and easily discernible in renal disease, but the opposite condition, sodium depletion or clinical dehydration, is more commonly the result of vomiting and diarrhea when they are complications of terminal renal disease. Sodium and water depletion can be recognized by a lack of elasticity in the superficial tissues and by poor filling of the blood vessels, as well as by signs of impaired circulation, including a fall in blood pressure and an increase in pulse rate. Though changes in intracellular fluid volume occur in some diseases, especially when the potassium content of the body is affected, there is no easy way of detecting them.

Because of the importance of osmotic forces in determining fluid distribution within the body, an important attribute of body fluid is its overall osmotic concentration, or osmolality. This depends on the concentration of solutes. While all solutes contribute to osmolality, small particles such as sodium or chloride ions are influential out of all proportion to their weight, and indeed account for over 90 percent of the osmolality of plasma. In the context of renal disease, changes in osmolality depend largely on how the kidney handles water. When the kidney either is incapable of conserving water or is not stimulated by vasopressin of the pituitary to do so, water is lost from the body, and a state of water depletion develops, characterized by increasing osmolality of body fluid. At other times, the kidneys may retain too much water, especially when too much hormone is present. In this case, water excess results, giving a clinical state of water intoxication, with decreased osmolality of body fluids.

Another important general property of body fluid is its degree of acidity or alkalinity. The kidneys are involved in the excretion of hydrogen ions, and imperfect function leads to their retention, the state of so-called renal acidosis. Renal acidosis may occur as part of general renal failure or as a specific disease of the renal tubules, one of whose functions is to convert the slightly alkaline glomerular filtrate into the (usually) acidic urine.

Apart from these general changes in body fluid, the pattern of individual constituents can be distorted in renal disease. For many substances, the problem is one of failure of excretion, with consequent increased concentration in body fluids. Insofar as excretion is achieved by filtration, the rise in concentration may assist excretion, permitting prolonged states of balance, at the cost of increased, but often tolerable, levels of concentration. For example, an individual in renal failure must put out as much urea as a healthy individual taking the same diet. But that person can only do so at a blood-urea concentration of 100 mg per 100 ml, instead of a normal blood-urea of 25 mg per 100 ml. Substances whose concentration increases in this way include urea, creatinine, uric acid, phosphate, sulfate, urochrome, and indeed all the usual constituents of urine apart from those that are "regulated" rather than simply "excreted."

Potassium should be mentioned because of the special danger associated with its retention, which can lead to fatal irregularity of cardiac action. This is a recognized danger of acute renal failure, now commonly prevented by use of the artificial kidney and its semipermeable membranes, and sometimes by the use of resins that will take up potassium in the alimentary tract.

Normal urine contains traces of protein, and in many forms of renal disease there is an increased excretion of protein in the urine, usually representing an increased permeability of the tuft of capillaries forming the glomerulus. This increased proteinuria (often, but less correctly, known as albuminuria) generally amounts to 0.5 gram (about 0.02 ounce) per day or more. When it exceeds 5 grams (about 0.2 ounce) per day and persists at this level, the loss of protein in the urine exceeds the capacity of the liver to produce new protein from the available materials. The concentration of protein in the blood decreases, and this leads to an increasing outflow of fluid from the bloodstream into the tissues (there is normally an equilibrium between the physical pressure in the capillaries, which tends to force fluids out, and the osmotic pressure of plasma proteins, the effect of which is to hold fluid in). This balance of forces is upset by a deficit of plasma proteins. The general loss of fluid into the tissues leads to massive edema, to which the kidneys contribute further by retaining salt and water. The combination of high levels of protein in the urine, low protein levels in the blood, and consequent edema is known as the nephrotic syndrome. This is a good example of a syndrome, defined as a recognizable pattern of manifestations that has not one but a number of possible causes. Other examples of syndromes in renal disease are acute renal failure and chronic renal failure.

DEHYDRATION

Dehydration is the excessive loss of water from the body. It is almost invariably associated with some loss of salt (sodium chloride) as well. The treatment of any form of dehydration, therefore, requires not only the replacement of the water lost from the body but also the restoration of the normal concentration of salt within the body fluid.

Dehydration may be caused by restricted water intake, excessive water loss, or both. The most common cause of dehydration is failure to drink liquids. The deprivation of water is far more serious than the deprivation of food. The average person loses approximately 2.5 percent of total body water per day (about 1,200 ml [1.25 quarts]) in urine, in expired air, by insensible perspiration, and from the gastrointestinal tract. If, in addition to this loss, the loss through perspiration is greatly increased—as is demonstrated in the case of the shipwrecked sailor in tropical seas or the traveler lost in the desert—dehydration may result in shock and death within only a few hours. When swallowing is difficult in extremely ill persons, or when people cannot respond to a sense of thirst because of age or illness or dulling of consciousness, the failure to compensate for the daily loss of body water will result rapidly in dehydration and its consequences. Large volumes of water also may be lost from the body by vomiting or diarrhea.

The symptoms of dehydration depend in part on the cause and in part on whether there is associated salt deprivation as well. When loss of water is disproportionately greater than loss of electrolytes (salt), the osmotic pressure of the extracellular fluids becomes higher than in the cells. Since water passes from a region of lower to a region of higher osmotic pressure, water flows out of the cells into the extracellular fluid, tending to lower its osmotic pressure and increase its volume toward normal. As a result of the flow of water out of the cells, they become dehydrated. This results in the thirst that always accompanies "pure" water depletion.

In those diseases in which there is loss of salt in excess of water loss, the decreased concentration of sodium in the extracellular fluid and in the blood serum results in decreased osmotic pressure, and water therefore enters the cells to equalize the osmotic pressure. Thus there is extracellular dehydration and intercellular hydration— and no thirst.

A Pakistani girl collecting water from a hand pump. Maintaining hydration is fundamental for health. Arif Ali/AFP/Getty Images

Water deprivation produces distinctive symptoms in humans. Weight loss, amounting to .9 to 1.36 kg (2 to 3 pounds) per day, occurs. Thirst is the most prominent symptom, with the dryness of mouth, decreased production of saliva, and impaired swallowing that accompany it. It is probable that thirst is the result of this subsequent intracellular dehydration and increased intracellular osmotic pressure. Experimentally, thirst can be produced when the cells have lost about 1 percent of their intracellular water.

As dehydration progresses, the tissues tend to shrink, the skin becomes dry and wrinkled, and the eyes become sunken and the eyeballs soft. Fever develops, possibly from mild to marked, as dehydration progresses. Dehydration itself probably affects the temperature regulatory centres in the brain. As dehydration and salt loss progress, however, the plasma volume and heart output decrease, with a consequent decrease in blood supply to the skin. Sweating decreases and may stop completely, and the main avenue for heat loss is closed. The body temperature may then rise precipitously.

There are marked changes in the volume of the extracellular and intracellular fluids, but the blood plasma volume changes the last and the least. The plasma volume is maintained more or less constant at the expense of the tissue fluids. If, however, the plasma volume does fall, the output of the heart also falls, and the pulse rate climbs, all of which indicates a dangerous physical state.

The renal changes that occur in humans during prolonged water depletion similarly tend to maintain a normal balance. If water deprivation continues and the plasma volume falls, however, the output of urine will be drastically reduced. As long as urine output of more than 30 ml (1 ounce) per hour is maintained, the kidney can excrete nitrogenous and nonnitrogenous solids with maximum efficiency. Once the urine flow is decreased below this level, the kidney is unable to function efficiently, the substances are retained in the body, and their concentration in the blood rises.

The final result of prolonged dehydration is now apparent. The normal distribution of salt and water in the body is destroyed, the plasma volume decreases, and the blood viscosity increases. As a result of these changes renal function is impaired, the urinary output falls, and waste products accumulate. Far more life-threatening, however, is decreased loss of moisture from the skin, with the subsequent rise in temperature, and the fall in cardiac output with the attendant irreversible shock.

Once renal failure occurs, about 8 percent of the total body water has been lost (4 litres [about 4.25 quarts]). When 5 to 10 litres (about 5.25 to 10.5 quarts) of body water have been lost, a person is acutely and severely ill, with contracted plasma volume, increased concentration and viscosity of the blood, renal failure and excessive urea in the blood, and falling blood pressure. In a previously healthy adult, death follows the loss of 12 to 15 litres (about 12.5 to 15.8 quarts) of body water. In the very young, the very old, or the debilitated, death occurs at a lower level of dehydration.

The treatment of any form of dehydration depends not only on restoring the depleted water but also on reestablishing normal levels of body electrolytes and limiting the production of nitrogenous waste products. Before any of these therapeutic measures can be applied, however, the initiating cause must be removed. The sailor or the desert traveler must be rescued, the vomiting infant must be cured, or the underlying disease must be treated. Then, after accurate biochemical determinations of the levels of various electrolytes and other blood components have been made and the plasma volume has been measured, the physician may give measured quantities of the appropriate mixtures of salt and water. Given the right amounts of salt and water, the human body will gradually restore the normal relationships between the cells, the extracellular fluid, and the plasma volume. That done, the complicated functions of the kidney will clear the circulating blood of the retained waste products, and the body will have restored its own normal balance.

DIABETES INSIPIDUS

Diabetes insipidus is a pathological endocrine condition characterized by excessive thirst and excessive production of very dilute urine. The disorder is caused by a lack of vasopressin (antidiuretic hormone) or a blocking of its action. This hormone, produced by the hypothalamus, regulates the kidney's conservation of water and production of urine through its ability to stimulate reabsorption of water by the kidneys. Diabetes insipidus is so named because the large volume of urine that is excreted is tasteless, or "insipid," rather than sweet, as is the case in diabetes mellitus, in which the urine may contain large quantities of glucose.

Diabetes insipidus may be caused by a deficiency of vasopressin secretion (central diabetes insipidus) or by a deficiency of vasopressin action in the kidney (nephrogenic diabetes insipidus). The form of the disorder that results from injury to the hypothalamic nucleus, which is the tract by which vasopressin is conveyed to the neurohypophysis (posterior lobe of the pituitary gland) for storage, is called central diabetes insipidus. This condition may be caused by trauma, such as brain or pituitary surgery, and diseases, such as brain tumours, pituitary tumours, or granulomatous infiltration (formation of grainlike lumps that are associated with certain diseases, including tuberculosis and sarcoidosis).

When a result of trauma, the condition only occurs if about 90 percent or more of the neurohypophyseal system (in the posterior lobe of the pituitary gland) is destroyed. Central diabetes insipidus also can be caused by mutations in the genes encoding vasopressin and neurophysin (a protein synthesized by the hypothalamus) that result in decreased production of vasopressin. In some patients, however, no cause can be found, and the condition is called idiopathic central diabetes insipidus.

Another form of the disease is called nephrogenic diabetes insipidus, which results when the supplies of vasopressin are adequate but the kidney tubules are unresponsive—either genetically or because of an acquired condition. The most severe form of this disorder is congenital hereditary nephrogenic diabetes insipidus. This condition is caused by mutations in a gene designated *AVPR2* (arginine vasopressin receptor 2), which encodes a specific form of the vasopressin receptor, or by mutations in a gene known as *AQP2* (aquaporin 2), which encodes a specific form of aquaporin. The vasopressin receptor gene *AVPR2* is located on the X chromosome. As a result, affected males have notably more-severe diabetes insipidus than do females.

Acquired nephrogenic diabetes insipidus can occur in patients with electrolyte imbalances, such as high serum calcium concentrations or low serum potassium concentrations, in patients with kidney disease, and in patients taking lithium carbonate. Acquired nephrogenic diabetes insipidus is rarely severe, and patients have normal vasopressin secretion, making treatment with desmopressin (a chemically modified form of vasopressin) ineffective. Adequate fluid must be provided, although the volume needed can be minimized somewhat if salt intake is limited or a diuretic drug is administered.

The symptoms of both forms of diabetes insipidus are similar and include excessive thirst and excretion of large volumes of urine—usually 3 to 6 litres (about 3.2 to 6.3 quarts) each day, although up to 20 litres (21.1 quarts) per day has been recorded. Water is the preferred fluid, and, if it or other fluid is freely available, patients remain well except for the inconvenience of frequent drinking and urination day and night. In the absence of a source of fluid, patients become increasingly thirsty and irritable and ultimately stuporous and comatose as a result of hyperosmolality and decreased extracellular fluid volume.

Diagnosis of central diabetes insipidus is based on the presence of high serum osmolality and low urine osmolality and on the results of a fluid deprivation test, with measurements of serum osmolality and urine output and urine osmolality when fluids are restricted. During a fluid deprivation test, patients with diabetes insipidus continue to excrete large volumes of urine, and administration of vasopressin causes a decrease in urine volume, an increase in urine osmolality, and a decrease in serum osmolality. In contrast, in nephrogenic diabetes insipidus there is no response to administration of vasopressin.

Central diabetes insipidus can be treated effectively using desmopressin, which can be given by nasal spray, tablet, or injection. Injections of vasopressin are ineffective for those with nephrogenic diabetes insipidus.

SYNDROME OF INAPPROPRIATE ANTIDIURETIC HORMONE

Syndrome of inappropriate antidiuretic hormone, or SIADH, is a disorder characterized by the excessive excretion of sodium in the urine, thereby causing hyponatremia (decreased sodium concentrations in the blood plasma). SIADH is caused by excessive unregulated secretion of vasopressin. In this syndrome, vasopressin secretion is inappropriate because it is not stimulated by high serum concentrations of solutes (high osmolality) or by low plasma volume—the factors that normally activate the hypothalamus and thereby trigger pituitary release of the hormone. The excess vasopressin stimulates reabsorption of water by the kidneys, which results in an increase in the volume of extracellular fluid and a decrease in the serum concentrations of sodium, chloride, and other substances. These processes result in the production of concentrated urine and are a reflection of vasopressin activity.

There are no tumours of the posterior pituitary that secrete excess amounts of vasopressin. However, other tumours, particularly those of the lung, may secrete large amounts of vasopressin, causing SIADH. Other causes of excess vasopressin secretion include brain tumours, other central nervous system disorders, adrenocorticotropic hormone deficiency, and several drugs (such as opiates, carbamazepine, and several anticancer drugs). Each of these conditions can result in activation of the hypothalamic-posterior pituitary system and stimulation of vasopressin release independent of the usual regulatory factors.

The onset of symptoms may be acute or chronic, with sudden or gradual loss of appetite, nausea and vomiting, sleepiness, confusion and disorientation, and ultimately seizures, coma, and death. When the onset is very slow, there may be few or even no symptoms.

Initial treatment for SIADH typically involves restriction of water intake and eradication of the underlying cause, if known. Patients with very low serum sodium concentrations can be treated by intravenous administration of concentrated salt solutions along with a diuretic. This allows the serum concentration of solutes to increase and the plasma volume to decrease.

VASCULAR DISEASE AND RENAL FUNCTION

Primary vascular disease—disease affecting the blood vessels—is sometimes a cause of renal damage. The most dramatic instance of this is the condition known as malignant hypertension, or accelerated hypertension, which arises when the blood pressure attains extremely high levels, the diastolic figure (the blood pressure between heart contractions) being 140 mmHg or higher (the normal being around 80 mmHg). Sustained levels of this magnitude cause serious damage to the arterioles, the smallest of the arteries. This damage is widespread, but as it affects the kidneys it produces rapid destruction of renal substance, with a scarred kidney. Unless the blood pressure is controlled, malignant hypertension can cause death in a few months. Since treatment at an early stage is notably effective, the condition represents an important medical emergency. Since the retinas are damaged as rapidly as the kidneys, the affected person may first notice blurring or loss of vision and will typically have a severe headache. Prompt treatment is necessary to avoid stroke, as well as damage to other organs.

More modest, but still elevated, levels of blood pressure can cause more gradual renal damage in elderly people or in those made prematurely aged by widespread arteriosclerosis ("hardening of the arteries"). In this condition the damage is in the larger arteries rather than in the arterioles, and the condition is one of slowly progressive scarring. Renal damage can also arise, by various mechanisms, in a large number of diseases that impair the proper functioning of the blood vessels, such as diabetes mellitus, the collagen disorders, bacterial inflammation of the heart lining, and many more.

A specific renovascular cause of high blood pressure that, although uncommon, is important from the point of view of the control of blood pressure in healthy individuals involves the juxtaglomerular apparatus and the secretion of renin. Occasionally, following trauma or arising spontaneously as a result of vascular disease, one or the other of the main renal arteries becomes constricted (renal artery stenosis). The fall in blood pressure beyond the constriction leads to increased secretion of renin from the juxtaglomerular apparatus with the formation of the vasoactive angiotensin II. As a result, the blood pressure rises. Removal of the affected kidney, surgical repair of the constriction, or percutaneous transluminal angioplasty (a balloon catheter inserted through the skin and inflated in the artery to flatten plaque buildup) usually restores the blood pressure and the blood renin level to normal.

DISORDERS OF URINE FLOW

If little or no urine appears, it may be because the kidneys are forming little urine (oliguria) or none (anuria), or it may represent a holdup in the bladder or urethra affecting the outflow from both kidneys. About one person in 500 is born with only one kidney, and loss of a kidney from disease or accident is not rare. The loss of a single kidney does not substantially affect an individual's ability to eliminate wastes, as long as the other kidney functions normally. In cases in which complete obstruction of the remaining ureter occurs, patients will experience effects similar to obstruction of the entire lower urinary tract. Partial or complete failure to form urine is treated in the section on acute renal failure, obstructive conditions in the section on diseases of the urinary tract.

In instances of damage to nervous control, certain typical clinical situations may be differentiated, corresponding to different modes of disordered urinary flow: (1) Lack of conscious inhibition of micturition because of damage to the cerebral cortex or, more commonly, from psychological causes results in a need to micturate that cannot be suppressed even though the bladder volume may be quite small. Micturition is precipitate and continues until the bladder is empty. (2) Transverse lesions or other damage to the spinal cord above the sacral reflex centres that cause paralysis of the lower half of the body produce at first a bladder that is atonic (lacking in physiological tone). This bladder becomes greatly distended, and the detrusor relaxes and reflex micturition is abolished. Pressure finally rises sufficiently to overcome the spasm of the sphincters and urine is voided in small amounts. Further accumulation and partial voiding of the overflow recur (overflow incontinence). Under these conditions the bladder readily becomes inflamed, which may cause disability or death from chronic ascending urinary infection. Intermittent drainage of the bladder with a catheter may be necessary, or firm pressure on the lower abdominal wall may be used to avoid overdistension and to develop an "automatic" bladder after some time. This is a small capacity organ (around 150 ml, or 5 fluid ounces) with frequent emptying. There is reflex control mediated through the sacral segments of the spinal cord. The higher centres do not restrain the detrusor, and the internal sphincter relaxes more readily. Voluntary assistance from the abdominal muscles helps in this situation if these too have not been paralyzed. There is, however, always some residual urine from incomplete emptying and a risk of infection. In some cases, pressure building within the bladder can be transmitted to the kidneys. Without medications or more frequent bladder emptying to relieve the pressure, the kidneys will incur damage. (3) In contrast, there is the isolated, or "autonomous," bladder resulting from damage to the central nervous system below the sacral cord reflex centres or to the nerves supplying the bladder and urethra. The bladder becomes tense but contracts only weakly so that, while small amounts of urine are voided, the residual urine may be as high as 200–300 ml (6.8–10.1 fluid ounces). This condition is known as active incontinence as opposed to the overflow incontinence of the automatic bladder. Here again, more effective emptying of the bladder by catheter drainage may be helpful.

Pain associated with urination (dysuria) can arise from bladder distension, which is then relieved by effective micturition; from inflammation of the lower urinary tract, commonly due to infection but rarely caused by chemical irritants in the urine; and from mechanical irritation by tumour or during the passage of stones. Dysuria is commonly, but not necessarily, associated with frequency of urination. This in turn may represent either an irritable or contracted bladder; or the actual amount of urine formed may be unusually large (polyuria), in which case voiding is likely to be painless. Sometimes polyuria may not be noticed by day but may manifest itself in the need to micturate on several occasions during the night (nocturia). The acute onset of dysuria and frequency suggests urinary infection. Sustained polyuria is more likely to be due to renal failure (defective concentrating power) or to diabetes. In those who drink beverages into the night, nocturia is physiological.

Incontinence, the involuntary passage of urine (or feces), may be due to a faulty nerve supply, which either leaves the sphincters relaxed or allows them to be overcome by distension of the bladder. Comatose and disturbed patients, especially among the elderly, are commonly incontinent. Apart from nerve lesions, the sphincters that normally prevent the escape of urine may be damaged by repeated childbirth, by the growth of the prostate, or by other distortions of the bladder neck. Medications to relax the bladder and increase its capacity may be helpful. Alternately, more complete bladder emptying by intermittent catheterization may limit the amount of urine leakage. Procedures have been devised to stimulate the sphincters electrically, when their nerve supply is damaged, or to stimulate the bladder to empty itself at set times. For chronic incontinence, however, devices to catch the urine and prevent soiling of clothing are the most practical.

OBSTRUCTION TO THE FLOW OF URINE

Urinary obstruction of the kidney (obstructive nephropathy) may arise at the junction of the renal pelvis and the ureter, either from faulty action of smooth muscle or from the pressure of an abnormal blood vessel crossing the pelvis. Such cases can benefit from a plastic operation on the renal pelvis or from division of the abnormal vessel. Whether the obstruction arises in this way, or lower down, it can lead to renal pain, to the passage of irregular amounts of urine when obstruction is intermittent, and to a mass in the kidney when obstruction persists. As the renal pelvis swells, the renal tissue shrinks, leading to the condition called hydronephrosis, in which a greatly swollen sac is surrounded by a mere rind of atrophied renal tissue. A massive hydronephrosis, with negligible renal substance remaining, may suggest removal of the kidney.

The kidney may be wounded, usually along with other viscera. In some cases it may be bruised, or it may even be ruptured in closed injuries. Since the kidney receives about a fifth of the blood pumped by the heart, bleeding can be profuse, both into the urine and into the tissues and the kidney, forming a large mass of blood, called a hematoma, and leading to surgical shock. Some bleeding may follow the procedure of renal biopsy (taking a specimen of kidney tissue for examination), but with proper precautions this is not severe. In the past, massive irradiation to the kidney region led to chronic renal damage (radiation nephritis), but with adequate precautions, this is no longer so.

The usual signs of traumatic injury to the kidney are blood in the urine and the development of a tender mass in the loin, with progressive signs of shock (pallor, sweating, fall in blood pressure). Such signs call for resuscitation and for surgical exploration if the bleeding continues. The surgical treatment may be carried out to arrest the bleeding by closing the tear. The kidney must be surgically removed if it cannot be saved. Abnormal solitary kidneys are not unknown, and such kidneys are more exposed to trauma by their size or position. Removal of such a kidney can lead only to death unless transplantation is possible.

While it is possible for the urinary tract to be obstructed by a large mass

A medieval surgeon removing a bladder stone. Hulton Archive/Getty Images

(tumour, stone, or foreign body) lying in the bladder, the tubular portions of the tract (urethra and ureters) are much more vulnerable to obstruction. The urethra may be obstructed by stones (calculi) formed in the bladder or kidneys; by fibrous contraction of the urethral wall (urethral stricture); and by congenital valve or diaphragm (membranous malformation). Although not a part of the excretory tract, the prostate lies close to the bladder neck, and in older men it is an important cause of obstruction. Fibrous disease of the bladder neck can also cause obstruction. The ureters can likewise be obstructed by calculi and stricture (narrowing); by fibrosis — scarring — of surrounding tissue (retroperitoneal fibrosis); and by tumour, though this is more likely to cause blood in the urine (hematuria).

Urinary calculi vary greatly in size. Mostly they contain calcium phosphate, calcium oxalate, uric acid, or cystine. Predisposing factors include infection, a high rate of calcium excretion, a low rate of urine formation, and various metabolic disorders, notably gout. They may cause trouble by their size or by entering the ureter or urethra, giving rise to colic, to hematuria, and, in the event of impaction, to obstructive kidney disease. The direct treatment of calculi is surgical, but sometimes the stone can be fragmented in situ by a lithotriptor. The sufferer needs general investigation for any underlying cause (e.g., a functioning parathyroid tumour that causes excessive excretion of calcium).

In the past at least, a common cause of urethral stricture was gonorrhea, in which inflammation of the urethra is followed by scarring and stricture. Bruising of the urethra by instruments during treatment can also occur. The affected person has increasing difficulty in passing urine, and the bladder becomes distended. Treatment may be either by repeated dilation of the stricture or by surgery.

KIDNEY STONES

Kidney stones (or renal calculi) are concretions of minerals and organic matter that form in the kidneys. Such stones may become so large as to impair normal renal function. Urine contains many salts in solution, and if the concentration of mineral salts becomes excessive, the excess salt precipitates as crystals that may enlarge to become visible, solid particles called stones. Kidney stones are classified as primary if they form without apparent cause, such as an infection or obstruction. They are classified as secondary if they develop after a renal infection or disorder.

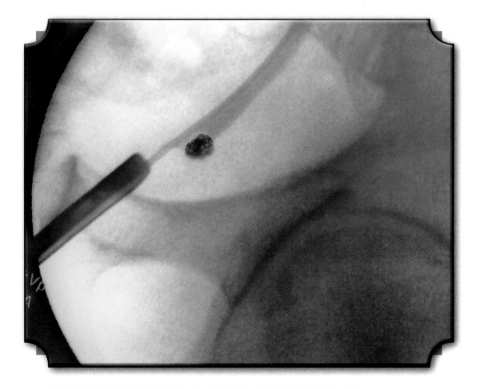

An X-ray of a kidney stone. iStockphoto/Thinkstock

Certain circumstances increase the likelihood of stone formation. Either a reduction in fluid volume or a surge in mineral concentration can be enough to upset the delicate balance between the liquid and its solutes. An increase in mineral concentration in the kidneys may occur because of metabolic conditions or infections. Once a stone starts developing, it generally continues to grow. A nucleus for precipitation of urinary salts can be a clump of bacteria, degenerated tissue, sloughed-off cells, or a tiny blood clot. Minerals start collecting around the foreign particle and encrusting it. As the stone increases in size, the surface area available for additional mineral deposition is continually increased.

Kidney stones, if large, can obstruct the outflow of urine, allow infections to persist, and create spasms in the renal tubules, a condition known as renal colic. In renal colic there is generally severe pain leading from the kidneys down through the abdomen and groin. Stones may cause obstruction in the renal pelvis, in a ureter, or in the bladder.

Many persons with kidney stones fail to show distinct symptoms. Others, however, can have severe kidney pain, infection, and inflammation. The most severe pain occurs where the passage of urine from the kidney is obstructed by the stone. Treatment includes medications to clear up infections and to relieve pain. Some stones may dissolve, and most stones pass without active intervention. Large stones that fail to dissolve are removed by surgery.

Enuresis

Enuresis is an elimination disorder characterized by four factors: the repeated voluntary or involuntary voiding of urine during the day or night into bedding or clothing; two or more occurrences per month for a child between ages five and six (one or more for older children); chronological age of at least five, mental age of at least four; and the absence of a causative physical disorder. Enuresis may additionally be classified as primary (when urinary continence has never been achieved), secondary (when continence was achieved for at least one year and then lost), nocturnal (occurring only during sleep), or diurnal (occurring during waking hours). The most prevalent form is nocturnal enuresis (also called bed-wetting and usually of the primary type), and the disorder occurs more often among boys than girls. Roughly 1 percent of children continue to be affected by this disorder until the age of 18.

A number of genetic, social, physical, and psychological factors may play a role in the disorder. Considerable evidence indicates that enuretic individuals often are members of families in which parents or siblings also have been enuretic. Stressful life events, poor toilet training, and chronic social disadvantage are among the social factors that have been found to increase the prevalence of enuresis. No specific physical factor has been pinpointed, but slight delay in maturation and limited functional bladder capacity have been noted in some enuretic children. While some enuretic children have emotional or behavioral disorders, no causal relationship can be established with certainty.

Treatment includes education and reassurance of parents and child, behavioral-conditional therapy, and the use of an alarm to awaken the child when urination is begun. The latter treatment is often effective, as it allows the child with nocturnal enuresis to associate the presence of a full bladder with the need to awaken and go to the bathroom. Treatment by drugs is usually a last resort. Vasopressin, taken as a nasal spray, is effective at decreasing the amount of urine produced at night. The drug imipramine has had some success in increasing the bladder's capacity to hold urine, but no single method of treatment has been entirely successful.

URINARY TRACT INFECTION

A urinary tract infection (UTI) is an inflammation of the renal system that is characterized by frequent and painful urination. It is caused by the invasion of microorganisms, usually bacteria, into the urethra and bladder. Infection of the urinary tract can result in either minor or major illness. For example, an attack of cystitis—inflammation of the bladder—may cause only a small amount of pain and discomfort, whereas infection that spreads into the upper urinary tract may lead to acute complications, such as obstruction of the ureter and kidney failure, or to chronic conditions, such as incontinence or kidney scarring that gradually progresses to kidney failure. Severe or recurrent UTI can result in lifelong discomfort and decrease in quality of life.

RISK FACTORS

UTIs are very common and can occur in people of all ages. However, women are affected about 30 times more often than men. In fact, roughly one in five women experiences a UTI in her lifetime. Girls and women are at high risk of infection because of the short female urethra. In addition, sexual intercourse, especially when a diaphragm is used for contraception, and pregnancy, when there may be partial stagnation of the urine from pressure on the urinary tract, significantly increase the susceptibility of women to UTI.

Many women experience recurrent UTIs, and those who have had three or more infections are likely to have frequent recurrences throughout their lifetimes. It is unclear why some women are at high risk for repeated infection. There is evidence that certain antigens of the P blood group system that are expressed on the surfaces of cells lining the urinary tract act as adhesion sites for bacteria, thereby facilitating infection. Postmenopausal women may have recurrent UTIs because decreasing levels of estrogen cause thinning of the vaginal epithelium, thereby reducing defense against invasion by microorganisms.

Other populations at risk of infection include men over age 50, in whom onset of prostatic disease may lead to urinary infection. Infants also are at risk, since diapers can facilitate the entry of organisms into the urethra. In addition, people affected by kidney stones, diabetes, disorders of the immune system, and abnormalities of the renal system are at increased risk of infection. In some patients, the introduction of a catheter into the bladder may be necessary to relieve urethral obstruction. However, this procedure increases risk of UTI.

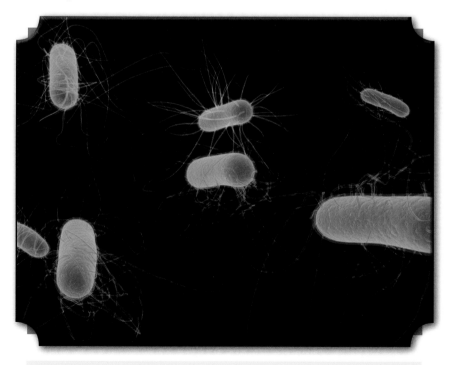

Illustration of E. coli *bacteria, the most common cause of urinary tract infection.* Hemera/Thinkstock

CAUSES

The most common cause of UTI is infection with *Escherichia coli*, a type of bacterium that normally inhabits the bowel, where it is relatively harmless. These organisms become a cause of UTI only when they enter the urethra.

The second most common bacterial cause of UTI is *Staphylococcus saprophyticus*, which normally occurs on the skin of some humans. Bacteria that are rare causes of UTIs but that may be involved in severe infections include *Proteus mirabilis* and organisms in the genera *Klebsiella*, *Mycoplasma*, *Enterococcus*, *Pseudomonas*, and *Serratia*. In rare cases, fungal organisms, such as *Candida* and *Coccidioides*, may be involved in complicated UTIs, which involve infection with multiple, different organisms. In addition, threadworms, flukes, and other parasites, as well as viruses such as HSV-2 (herpes simplex virus type 2) have been identified as infrequent causes of UTIs. Bacteria that cause UTIs are almost always transmitted during sexual intercourse, and thus proper hygiene of both partners is a useful way to prevent infection.

SYMPTOMS AND DIAGNOSIS

In all forms of urinary infection the urine may be cloudy and may contain more ammonia than usual. Urination tends to be painful if the urethra is inflamed. If the bladder is inflamed, urination is both painful and frequent. Bladder infection may cause fever, dull pain in the lower part of the abdomen, and vomiting. If the infection reaches the kidneys, symptoms are more severe, with pain in the loins, on one or both sides, and fever.

UTI is usually diagnosed based on symptoms, physical examination, and laboratory examination of the urine. In men, physical examination is important for detecting possible infection of the genitals and enlargement of the prostate gland, which may be a sign of serious disease. A clean-catch urine sample, in which urine is collected in midstream to prevent contamination with organisms present at the opening of the urethra, is necessary for laboratory analysis. Analysis may involve simple detection for the presence of bacteria, or it may involve culture and identification of the specific organism that is causing infection. Over-the-counter dipstick tests performed at home are useful for women who experience recurrent UTIs. These tests are based on the detection of nitrates such as those of ammonia in the urine.

In severe infections, laboratory culture of urine is required to identify the organism involved. Infections that extend into the kidneys may require examination using ultrasound or other visualization techniques, such as X-ray or computed tomography (CT) scanning. Blood analysis also may be performed to determine if infection has spread into the bloodstream, placing other tissues at risk. Recurrent infections may necessitate cystoscopy, in which an instrument called a cystoscope is inserted into the urethra and bladder to view the tissues and to collect samples for biopsy. In many cases, the extent of pyelonephritis (inflammation in the kidney and the lining of the renal pelvis) that is a direct result of recurrent UTI is not known with certainty. However, it is known that, in the presence of urinary tract obstruction, which disrupts the flow of urine, infection is likely to ascend the urinary tract and cause infection within the renal pelvis and kidney tissue.

TREATMENT

UTI is usually treated with sulfonamides or other anti-biotics, such as amoxicillin, ciprofloxacin, ampicillin, or nitrofurantoin. In addition, an analgesic (pain-relieving) agent such as pyridium is typically prescribed to reduce pain during urination. Recurrent infections often require long-term antibiotic therapy. However, in acute cases involving obstruction of the ureter, infection cannot be successfully eradicated by antibiotics until the obstruction is removed. In some cases, women with recurrent UTI may be given an antibiotic to take immediately following sexual intercourse in order to prevent infection. Postmenopausal women who experience frequent UTIs may benefit from the use of a vaginal estrogen cream that prevents thinning of the vaginal epithelium.

OTHER FACTORS IN URINARY TRACT DISEASE

In addition to the discrete diseases and disorders already described, there are certain other factors that cause or serve as indications of damage to the urinary tract. For example, hematuria, or the presence of blood in the urine, is a symptom of an underlying condition and is not in itself a cause of urinary tract disease. A variety of conditions can produce hematuria, and usually only through thorough examination and testing can its cause be identified. In contrast, in the case of trauma to the urinary tract, prompt medical care is required if the tissues are to have a chance at functional recovery, leaving little time for extensive diagnostic work prior to emergency surgical operations.

HEMATURIA

Hematuria (or haematuria), the presence of blood in the urine, is an indication of injury or disease of the kidney or some other structure of the urinary tract. In males blood in the urine can also come from the reproductive tract. The blood may become apparent during urination or only upon microscopic examination. Rarely, blood may appear in the urine in the absence of genito-urinary disease. Such instances may result from transfusion of incompatible blood, from severe burns, from abnormal blood conditions in which the red blood cells are broken down, or from blackwater fever (a complication of malaria).

Blood in the urine ordinarily comes from the urethra, the bladder, or the kidneys. When the urethra is involved, the blood appears at the start of urination and is bright red. The urethra may bleed because of physical injuries, obstructions, infections, or strictures (abnormally narrow sections). Blood coming from the bladder may contain clots and usually appears toward the end of urination. Such bleeding is usually caused by stones or tumours in the bladder. In persons who are tuberculous, blood may come from ulcers in the bladder wall. In even rarer cases, a vein in the bladder wall may distend and rupture, causing hemorrhages. Parasites such as blood flukes may burrow into the bladder wall and cause bleeding.

Renal (kidney) bleeding can be produced by a number of disorders, including ruptured blood vessels, tumours, renal obstructions, kidney stones, chemical irritants (e.g., carbon tetrachloride, lead compounds, and ethylene glycol), and infections and inflammation of the kidney (e.g., Bright disease, pyelonephritis). In some cases there may be excessive bleeding from the kidneys with no apparent cause. Hematuria unaccompanied by pain is ordinarily regarded as due to a tumour in the urinary tract until proved otherwise.

TRAUMA

Apart from the urethra, the urinary tract is likely to be injured only in massive general injury or by accidental ligation (tying) of the ureters in a pelvic operation. The urethra can, however, be ruptured by a blow or fall on the perineum (crotch). If there is no external wound, the damage is indicated by the appearance of a swelling containing blood and urine, by the inability to pass urine, and by bleeding from the urethra. The patient may go into shock and requires urgent surgical repair of the urethra and drainage of the potentially infected swelling.

CHAPTER 5

KIDNEY FAILURE AND INFLAMMATORY AND MALIGNANT RENAL DISEASES AND DISORDERS

D amage to the kidneys, whether from inflammation, infection, tumours, or other conditions, results in the accumulation of fluid and waste products in the body. These abnormal changes often manifest physically as vomiting, weakness, shortness of breath, and swelling in the face, hands, or ankles. If left untreated, a complete loss of renal function may ensue. Hence, diseases and disorders affecting the kidneys represent a set of serious and potentially fatal conditions.

In addition to classification by disease type, such as whether the condition is infectious or malignant (cancerous), diseases and disorders of the kidney can also be classified according to other criteria, such as whether they arise from causes that are primary or secondary in nature. Primary disorders originate in the renal system itself, such as when a genetic variation directly alters the structure or function of the kidneys. In contrast, secondary disease occurs when disease that originated elsewhere in the body alters renal function through indirect mechanisms. Diseases and disorders of the kidneys may be further distinguished by onset—whether acute (sudden) or chronic or occurring in childhood or adulthood. Examples of conditions included in this diverse assembly of kidney diseases and disorders are kidney failure, Bright disease, Bartter syndrome, and nephropathy.

KIDNEY FAILURE

Kidney, or renal, failure is the partial or complete loss of kidney function. Kidney failure is classified as acute or chronic. In the case of acute kidney failure, the affected person recovers usually in six weeks or less. In contrast, chronic renal failure is usually the result of prolonged diseases of the kidney. Chronically diseased kidneys can sustain life until about 90 percent of their functioning capacity has been lost.

ACUTE FAILURE

Acute renal failure occurs when renal function suddenly declines to very low levels, so that little or no urine is formed, and the substances, including even water, that the kidney normally eliminates are retained in the body. There are two main mechanisms that can produce acute renal failure. When the cardiac output—the amount of blood pumped into the general circulation by the heart—is lowered by hemorrhage or by medical or surgical shock, the renal circulation is depressed to an even greater extent. This leads directly to inefficient excretion, but, more importantly still, the kidney tissue cannot withstand prolonged impairment of its blood supply and undergoes either patchy or massive necrosis (tissue death).

Given time, the kidney tissue may regenerate, and it is on this hope that the treatment of acute renal failure is based. The form of acute renal failure that is due to a poor supply of blood (ischemia) has many causes, the most common and most important being multiple injuries, septicemia (infections invading the bloodstream), abortion with abnormal or excessive bleeding from the female genital tract, internal or external hemorrhage, loss of fluid from the body as in severe diarrhea or burns, transfusion reactions, and severe heart attacks. A special case is the transplanted kidney, which commonly goes through a phase of acute renal failure that is independent of possible rejection.

A Bangladeshi woman beside an arsenic filter. Poisons such as arsenic can cause acute renal failure. AFP/Getty Images

The second common mechanism of acute renal failure is toxic. Many poisons are excreted by the kidney, and in the process, like other urinary constituents, they become concentrated and thus reach levels in the tubular fluid that damage the lining cells of the tubules. Though the tubular cells die and are shed in the urine, regeneration can take place and the patient survive, if he can be maintained during the period of depressed renal function and is not killed by other effects of the poison. Poisons that can affect the kidney in this way are numerous, but the main groups are heavy metals (mercury, arsenic, uranium), organic solvents (carbon tetrachloride, propylene glycol, methanol), other organic substances (aniline, phenindione, insecticides), and antibacterial agents (sulfonamides, aminoglycosides, amphotericin), and some fungi (e.g., *Amanita phalloides*).

In addition to the ischemic and toxic causes of acute renal failure, mention must be made of fulminating varieties of acute renal illnesses that are generally mild (e.g., acute glomerulonephritis) and of the acute form of immunologic rejection that can destroy a kidney irrevocably within minutes of transplantation. Another mechanism of acute renal failure is characterized by acute obstruction of the flow of urine from the kidneys. This condition is easily treated by restoring adequate urinary drainage from at least one kidney.

The course of acute renal failure can usefully be divided into three phases: an onset phase, a phase of established acute renal failure, and a recovery phase. In general, but not invariably, the second of these phases is characterized by a low output of urine (oliguria) and the third by an increasing urine output (polyuria). The onset phase is dominated by general illness, in which the episode of acute renal failure arises. At this stage there may be evidence of threatened renal damage such as blood in the urine or pain in the loins. At this early stage, renal damage may be reversible by prompt treatment of circulatory failure (e.g., by the transfusion of adequate amounts of plasma, whole blood, or electrolyte replacement fluids) and by maintaining adequate blood oxygen levels. Infection or any underlying causative disorder also must be treated quickly.

In the second phase, small amounts of urine, often containing red blood cells, or hemoglobin, are passed. Complete absence of urine is not common and suggests that an obstruction is preventing urine from being passed. In quantitative terms, a urine volume of less than 500 ml (0.53 quarts) per day constitutes significant oliguria. This is the least amount in which the excretory demand imposed by an ordinary diet can be met. In the actual situation of acute renal failure, the excretory demands may in fact be much greater, since many of the causes of acute renal failure also are causes of increased breakdown of the tissues in general. The blood urea increases, the rate of increase being conditioned both by the degree of renal failure and by the amount of tissue breakdown. Besides nitrogen, the kidney can no longer excrete adequate amounts of water, sodium, and potassium.

These various inadequacies point the way to the necessary management of acute renal failure—the elimination from intake of any dangerous substance that the kidney can no longer handle. The diet must either be free of protein or contain small amounts of high-quality protein to lessen tissue breakdown. It must also be free from sodium and potassium: many persons with renal failure have died from pulmonary edema, a correlate of sodium retention, and others from the acute toxic effects on the heart of a raised level of potassium in the blood. Water cannot be excluded from the intake but must be limited to an amount estimated to equal the unavoidable loss of water from the skin and in breathing. The weight of the patient and the concentration of sodium in the blood are good guides to the adequacy of water restriction. In the absence of continuing losses of sodium from the body, as might occur from vomiting or diarrhea, a progressive fall in serum sodium implies that too much water is being taken in. Kidney function may recover, often in seven to 10 days. The use of dialysis, the removal of waste products by straining the blood through semipermeable membranes, gives further time for renal recovery. Potassium can be removed from the body by resins, but this is less often required if dialysis is available.

Although by comparison with the oliguric phase the recovery phase presents fewer problems, the convalescent kidney takes time to recover its full regulatory function, and electrolytes and water may be lost at an unusual rate during this stage, requiring replacement. Most individuals who survive completely recover from acute renal failure, but residual renal damage persists in some persons. In a few, this is so severe as to bring them effectively into the category of chronic renal failure. The artificial kidney has transformed the outlook for many patients with acute renal failure, and this, together with developments in the control of infection with more powerful antibiotics, constitutes one of the miracles of medicine in the last few decades.

CHRONIC FAILURE

The term *uremia*, though it is sometimes used as if it were interchangeable with chronic renal failure, really means an increase in the concentration of urea in the blood. This can arise in many acute illnesses in which the kidney is not primarily affected and also in the condition of acute renal failure described above. Uremia ought to represent a purely chemical statement, but it is sometimes used to denote a clinical picture, that of severe renal insufficiency.

As with acute renal failure, there are many conditions that can lead to chronic renal failure. The two most common causes are pyelonephritis and glomerulonephritis (kidney inflammation involving the structures around the renal pelvis or the glomeruli), and other common causes are renal damage from the effects of high blood pressure and renal damage from obstructive conditions of the lower urinary tract.

Primary disorders, such as pyelonephritis and glomerulonephritis, have in common a progressive destruction of nephrons, which may be reduced to less than a 20th of their normal number. The quantitative loss of nephrons can account for the majority of the changes observed in chronic renal failure. The failure in excretion is due directly to loss of glomerular filters, and other features such as the large quantities of dilute urine represent a change in tubular function that could be accounted for by the increased load that each remaining nephron has to carry. There are many other causes of chronic renal failure aside from the four common ones. They include congenital anomalies and hereditary disorders, diseases of connective tissue, tuberculosis, the effects of diabetes and other metabolic disorders, and a number of primary disorders of the kidney tubules. Of the many causes, there are some that have importance out of proportion to their frequency, by virtue of their reversibility. These include renal amyloidosis (abnormal deposits in the kidney of a complex protein substance called amyloid), whose causes may be treatable; damage to the kidney from excessive calcium or deficiency of potassium; uric acid deposition in gout; the effects of analgesic agents (substances taken to alleviate pain) and other toxic substances, including drugs.

The person suffering from renal failure, especially in the early stages, may have no symptoms other than a feeling of thirst and a tendency (shared with many normal people) to pass urine at frequent intervals and through the night. In other instances, the individual may be in a coma, with occasional convulsions. The general appearance of the sufferer may be sallow because of a combination of anemia and the retention of urinary pigment. Even if not in actual coma, the affected person may be withdrawn. Muscle twitchings and more general convulsions may occur. The coma is thought to represent poisoning, and convulsions are often related to the severity of the high blood pressure that commonly complicates advanced renal failure. Blurred vision is also a manifestation associated with high blood pressure. Bruising and hemorrhages may be noticeable.

The rapid improvement that follows dialysis points strongly to a toxic component. Urea itself is not notably toxic. Not all the chemical alterations in uremia are simple retentions. There is acidosis—a fall in the alkalinity of the blood and tissue fluids—reflected clinically in deep respiration as the lungs strive to eliminate carbon dioxide. The capacity of the kidney to adjust to variation in intake of salt, potassium, and water becomes progressively impaired, so that electrolyte disturbances are common. Poor appetite, nausea, vomiting, and diarrhea are common in uremic patients, and these in turn add another component to the chemical disturbance. Phosphate is retained in the blood and is thus associated with low blood levels of calcium. The parathyroids are overactive in renal failure, and vitamin D is less than normally effective because the kidneys manufacture less of its active form (1,25-dihydroxycholecalciferol). (Parathyroid hormone causes release of calcium from the bones, and vitamin D promotes absorption of calcium from the intestines.) These changes can lead to

A mother and son have their blood pressure checked at a local clinic. Suzy Allman/Getty Images

severe bone disease in persons suffering from renal failure, because bone calcium is depleted and the calcium stores are not adequately replenished.

In chronic renal failure, excessive production of renin by the kidney can lead to severe high blood pressure (hypertension), and the effects of this may even dominate the clinical picture. In addition to damage to the brain and the retina, the high blood pressure may lead directly to heart failure. Hypertension can also accelerate the progress of renal damage by its impact on the renal blood vessels themselves, setting up a cycle that can be hard to break. Anemia is also often severe due in part to a failure to produce erythropoietin.

The patient in advanced renal failure is vulnerable to infection and other complications, such as vomiting or diarrhea, which need special care. When symptoms of advanced renal failure appear, deterioration can be delayed by a strict low-protein diet, 18–20 grams (0.6–0.7 ounces) of high-quality protein each day. In terminal renal failure, the affected person can be rescued only by some form of dialysis and then maintained by dialysis or transplantation.

INFLAMMATORY DISEASES AFFECTING THE KIDNEYS

Inflammation is a response triggered by damage to living tissues that serves to localize and eliminate injurious agents and to remove damaged tissue components so that the body can begin to heal. Although inflammation is usually beneficial, it often causes unpleasant sensations. Prolonged or repeated inflammation in a tissue can lead to tissue damage and disordered function. Examples of important inflammatory diseases that affect the kidneys include Bright disease and pyelonephritis.

BRIGHT DISEASE

Bright disease, also known as glomerulonephritis, is an inflammation of the glomeruli and the nephrons of the kidney. In cases of glomerulonephritis, the glomeruli, the nephrons, and the tissues between nephrons are all afflicted.

Glomerulonephritis may be caused by disease states that disrupt the normal function of the immune system (e.g., systemic lupus erythematosus), compromise the structure or function of the systemic vasculature (e.g., inflammation of the arteries), or damage the glomeruli

Richard Bright. Hulton Archive/Getty Images

(e.g., high blood pressure [hypertension] or diabetic nephropathy). Glomerulonephritis can also arise from streptococcal infections such as strep throat. In some cases, however, a cause cannot be identified. Glomerulonephritis may occur only once or may recur. The successive stages of the disease are known as acute, subacute, and chronic.

Typically, glomerulonephritis appears as an acute illness one to two weeks after a sore throat, or—less commonly—after a persistent streptococcal infection of the skin. Acute glomerulonephritis is characterized by severe inflammation, renal insufficiency, increased blood pressure, and severe back pain. In this form of the disease, the kidneys are swollen, the capsule covering each kidney is taut and stretched, the surface is smooth and gray, and usually there are many small hemorrhages from the capillaries. The whole complex of glomeruli and nephrons swells. The illness is an alarming one, but the fact is that the acute attack of glomerulonephritis needs no particular treatment other than the eradication of the infection or withdrawal of the offending drug, with some restriction of fluid and protein. Hence, recovery is usually fairly complete after an episode of acute glomerulonephritis. However, minor infections may do further damage to the kidneys and bring on the subacute and chronic stages.

Subacute glomerulonephritis does not necessarily follow acute attacks. If it does develop, however, it has usually been preceded by an acute episode several months or years earlier. The kidney becomes considerably enlarged, the surface is smooth and pale, and the internal tissue is darker than normal. The paleness is due to the restriction of blood flow to the surface portion of the kidney and the high accumulation of fat (lipid) droplets. Bowman's capsules become filled with excess surface (epithelial) cells, red blood cells, and mineral crystals. The nephron tubules begin to degenerate. Because of the breakdown of kidney tissue, a greater amount of blood protein is lost into urine than should normally be released. Red blood cells forced through the constricted glomeruli become crushed, distorted, and fragmented. Their loss leads to anemia.

Chronic glomerulonephritis usually follows the other two stages, if the affected person survives long enough, but it has been found in a few individuals who apparently have not had previous kidney disease. In this stage the kidney is reduced mostly to scar tissue. It is small and shrivelled, and the surface is granular. Because the blood cannot be filtered of waste products, abnormal quantities of nitrogenous substances in the blood cause the condition known as uremia.

Treatment of all forms of glomerulonephritis is primarily directed toward controlling high blood pressure with antihypertensive (blood pressure-lowering) agents and diuretics and through changes in diet, which include fluid restriction and decreased salt intake. Some patients respond to treatment with anti-inflammatory drugs. Dialysis may be necessary to manage uremia.

In summary, glomerulonephritis can lead to renal failure within a few weeks or months, after many years of symptom-free proteinuria, or after a period of massive proteinuria, which causes the nephrotic syndrome. All of these manifestations may sometimes be seen in individuals who have never had, or cannot recall, an acute attack. Renal biopsies in many patients with glomerulonephritis show a range of glomerular reactions that include increased cellularity and basement membrane damage and thickening and varying degrees of progressive destruction of glomeruli. In those who recover, complete resolution of glomerular disease occurs.

A curious form of glomerulonephritis especially common in children is associated with little structural glomerular damage, at least as seen by the ordinary light microscope. Characteristic abnormalities affecting podocytes are revealed by electron microscopy. The condition is usually attended by heavy proteinuria and the nephrotic syndrome. Although the evidence for an immunologic cause of this form of glomerulonephritis is less certain than in other types, and the provoking antigen is unknown, paradoxically the disorder usually promptly resolves when the patient is treated with corticosteroids or other immunosuppressive drugs, and renal failure never occurs.

PYELONEPHRITIS

Pyelonephritis is an infection and inflammation of the kidney tissue and the renal pelvis. The infection is usually bacterial. The most common type of renal disorder, pyelonephritis may be chronic or acute.

Acute pyelonephritis generally affects one specific region of the kidney, leaving the rest of the kidney structure untouched. In many instances pyelonephritis develops without any apparent precipitating cause. Any obstruction to the flow of blood or urine, however, may make the kidneys more susceptible to infection, and fecal soiling of the urethral opening is thought to increase the incidence of the disease in infants (the urethra is the channel for urine from the bladder to the outside). Women may suffer injury of the urinary passages during intercourse or pregnancy, and catheterization (mechanical draining of urine) can cause infection.

In acute pyelonephritis the lining of the renal structures into which urine drains, the renal pelvis and the calyxes, may be inflamed. Abscesses may form in the kidney tissue, and some of the nephron tubules (urine-producing structures) may be destroyed. Medical treatment abates the infection over a period of one to three weeks. As healing takes place, scar tissue forms at the site of infection, but there is usually sufficient healthy tissue to maintain relatively normal renal functions. The symptoms of acute pyelonephritis usually include fever, chills, pain or aches in the lower back and flanks, bladder inflammation, tenderness in the kidney region, white blood cells in the urine, and a high urine bacterial count. Treatment usually requires suppression of bacterial growth by means of antibiotic drugs.

Chronic pyelonephritis results from bacterial infections in the kidneys over a period of years. Each episode of infection may pass unnoticed but may destroy more and more areas of tissue until the amount of functional kidney tissue is far less than the scar tissue that has formed. If only one kidney is involved or if the affected areas are limited, surgery may restore some functioning. Active infections are treated with antibacterial drugs. Frequently there is widespread and permanent destruction of renal tissue by the time the malady is discovered. Death can ensue from urine poisoning (uremia), severe current infections, or heart and vascular disorders precipitated by the renal condition. Use of artificial-kidney machines or a renal transplant can sometimes prolong life.

OTHER CONDITIONS AFFECTING THE KIDNEYS AND RENAL SYSTEM

Some disorders that affect kidney structure and function are hereditary, meaning that they are passed from parents to their offspring. These conditions range from inborn errors of metabolism, in which specific substances, such as certain amino acids, are excreted in excess, leading to disruptions in metabolite and fluid homeostasis in the body. Similar imbalances may arise from abnormalities in kidney structure. In addition, still other conditions affecting the kidneys arise from preexisting diseases, such as diabetes mellitus and high blood pressure (hypertension), which in some individuals are themselves associated with genetic factors.

BARTTER SYNDROME

Bartter syndrome, also called potassium wasting syndrome, is any of several rare disorders affecting the kidneys characterized primarily by the excessive excretion of potassium in the urine.

Bartter syndrome is named after American endocrinologist Frederic Bartter, who described the primary characteristics of the disorder in the early 1960s. Bartter examined two patients, both of whom had potassium deficiency (hypokalemia), abnormal increases in the number of cells (hyperplasia) of the juxtaglomerular apparatus of the kidneys, and high serum concentrations of the kidney enzyme renin. Bartter observed that these abnormalities were associated with resultant increases in angiotensin, as well as increases in the production of aldosterone. Increased production of aldosterone was subsequently associated with excessive potassium excretion. Because increased production of aldosterone is a central finding of Bartter syndrome, the disorder is recognized as a form of secondary hyperaldosteronism.

The onset of Bartter syndrome is usually in infancy or in childhood and may result in short stature and intellectual disability. Several genetic defects, primarily affecting potassium and chloride transport in the renal tubules, have been associated with the syndrome. The discovery of these mutations, occurring in different genes, has led to the stratification of Bartter syndrome into three main categories: neonatal Bartter syndrome, appearing in utero between 24 and 30 weeks of gestation; classic Bartter syndrome, appearing in infancy or early childhood; and Gitelman syndrome, appearing in late childhood or in adulthood.

There are two different types of neonatal Bartter syndrome, and these are clinically indistinguishable, even though they arise from mutations in different genes. Type 1 is caused by mutation of the gene designated *SLC12A1* (solute carrier family 12, member 1), whereas type 2 is caused by mutation of the gene *KCNJ1* (potassium inwardly rectifying channel, subfamily J, member 1). These genes play fundamental roles in maintaining physiological homeostasis of sodium and potassium concentrations.

Classic Bartter syndrome, or type 3, is caused by mutation in the gene known as *CLCNKB* (chloride channel Kb), which functions in the reabsorption of chloride and hence sodium in the kidney tubules. Mutations underlying classic Bartter syndrome result in the loss of function of the encoded protein, thereby leading to excessive excretion of sodium in the urine. This form of the syndrome appears to be hereditary. There also exists infantile Bartter syndrome with sensorineural deafness, or type 4, which arises from a combination of variations in *CLCNKB* and *CLCNKA* (chloride channel Ka) or from variation of the gene called *BSND* (Bartter syndrome, infantile, with sensorineural deafness).

Gitelman syndrome is caused by mutations in *SLC12A3* (solute carrier family 12, member 3), which encodes a protein that specializes in the transport of sodium and chloride into the kidney tubules, thereby mediating the reabsorption of these electrolytes and maintaining electrolyte homeostasis.

Bartter syndrome is diagnosed primarily on findings of increased potassium levels in the urine and increased concentrations of aldosterone and renin in the blood serum. Other findings may include metabolic alkalosis, which is a loss of acid from the body that arises from potassium and chloride depletion, and increased production and urinary excretion of prostaglandins, hormonelike substances that are derived from fatty acids. Diagnosis of Gitelman syndrome is based on findings similar to Bartter syndrome, as well as on hypomagnesemia, or abnormally low serum concentrations of magnesium, and hypocalciuria, or decreased levels of calcium in the urine.

Hypokalemia may be treated with potassium supplements, and additional supplements may be used to maintain sodium and other electrolyte concentrations. Other symptoms of Bartter syndrome may be reversed by drugs that inhibit the formation of prostaglandins, such as the anti-inflammatory agent indomethacin. Despite treatment, some patients may develop kidney failure.

CYSTINURIA

Cystinuria is a hereditary error of metabolism characterized by the excessive excretion into the urine of four amino acids: cystine, lysine, arginine, and ornithine. The main clinical problem of cystinuria is the possibility of cystine stone formation in the kidney. Unlike lysine, arginine, and ornithine, which are freely soluble, cystine is only slightly soluble in urine, and when urine volume decreases, particularly at night, this amino acid may form stones. These may be reduced or eliminated by forcing fluids, alkalization, or, in severe cases, dietary restriction of foods containing methionine and cystine.

Cystinuria is believed to be caused by a genetic defect in the transport system of the kidney tubule, which normally reabsorbs the four amino acids into the body circulation. In some forms of cystinuria, intestinal transport may be similarly affected. It is estimated that approximately one in 600 persons excretes abnormally large quantities of cystine, which can be detected by a simple test. Cystinuria is transmitted by an autosomal recessive gene: unaffected carriers of the trait who mate may expect, on the basis of chance, to have one affected offspring out of four.

DE TONI–FANCONI SYNDROME

De Toni–Fanconi syndrome is a metabolic disorder affecting kidney transport that is characterized by the failure of the kidney tubules to reabsorb water, phosphate, potassium, glucose, amino acids, and other substances. When the disorder is accompanied by cystinosis, a deposition of cystine crystals, it is called Fanconi syndrome. There is some variation, however, in the designation of these symptoms.

The de Toni–Fanconi syndrome results from injury to kidney tubular function, the primary injury being either hereditary or acquired (e.g., by repeated exposure to toxins). Treatment attempts to eliminate the primary cause. Phosphate and potassium supplements and adequate fluid intake also can help offset the disturbance in kidney transport, which may otherwise give rise to a softening of the bones, muscle weakness, and dehydration.

DIABETIC NEPHROPATHY

Diabetic nephropathy, also known as Kimmelstiel-Wilson disease (or diabetic glomerulosclerosis), is the deterioration of kidney function occurring as a complication of diabetes mellitus. The condition is characterized primarily by increased urinary excretion of the protein albumin, increased blood pressure, and reduced glomerular filtration rate (the average rate at which wastes are filtered out of the blood plasma by the kidneys). Diabetic nephropathy is a leading cause of end-stage renal disease (ESRD), which is characterized by kidney failure, with the organ's function reduced to less than one-tenth of normal capacity or lost completely.

Diabetic nephropathy generally manifests within 10 to 20 years of diabetes onset and affects roughly 20 to 40 percent of persons diagnosed with type I diabetes and 5 to 20 percent of those with type II diabetes. The disorder appears to cluster in families, particularly in those in which there exists a history of type I diabetes. This suggests that genetic factors might leave some diabetic individuals more susceptible to nephropathy than others. However, the underlying cause of the condition is unclear. A host of chronic pathological changes characteristic of diabetes have been implicated, including chronic high blood sugar (hyperglycemia), particularly when combined with high hypertension. Persistence of both conditions can result in damage to the nephrons.

There are five clinical stages of diabetic nephropathy. Progression from one stage to the next is determined by clinical measurements of blood pressure, urinary excretion of albumin, and glomerular filtration rate. The first stage, hyperfiltration, generally is considered to be an indication that the diabetic patient is at increased risk for nephropathy. Hyperfiltration is followed by normoalbuminuria, in which albumin excretion and blood pressure are normal but detectable glomerular lesions are present. The third stage, microalbuminuria, is characterized by elevations in blood pressure and urinary excretion of albumin and stable or decreasing glomerular filtration rate. Microalbuminuria generally appears 5 to 15 years following diabetes diagnosis. Stage four is known as overt albuminuria and is characterized by elevated urinary excretion of albumin (greater than 300 mg/ml, or more than 10 times normal), decreased glomerular filtration, and, in many patients, hypertension. Stage five, ESRD, ensues when the glomerular filtration rate drops below 15 ml per minute (the normal rate is 75–115 ml per minute for women and 85–125 ml per minute for men).

Treatment for diabetic nephropathy is focused primarily on the reduction of blood glucose levels and blood pressure. Although in many diabetic patients these factors can be controlled largely through diet and exercise, pharmacological interventions often are needed to prevent or

A person injecting himself with insulin. ©www.istockphoto.com/
Dr. Heinz Linke

delay the progression of diabetic nephropathy and to control the condition in severe cases. Pharmacological approaches to blood glucose management include the administration of insulin, which promotes the uptake of glucose from the blood by tissues such as muscle, and the use of oral hypoglycemic (blood glucose-lowering) medications, including sulfonylureas and thiazolidinediones.

These medications help limit the damage inflicted on renal blood vessels by harmful substances known as advanced glycation end products, which are formed from the union in the blood of glucose and the red blood cell component hemoglobin. Antihypertensive drugs used to delay the advance of diabetic nephropathy include angiotensin-converting enzyme inhibitors.

IMINOGLYCINURIA

Iminoglycinuria is an inborn impairment of the transport system of the kidney tubules, which normally reabsorb the amino acids glycine, proline, and hydroxyproline. In young children in whom this transport system fails to develop, high urinary levels of glycine, proline, and hydroxyproline have sometimes been observed in conjunction with convulsions, high cerebrospinal fluid protein, and intellectual disability. Other hereditary disorders affecting the transport of specific amino acids include the tryptophan malabsorption syndrome (or "blue diaper syndrome"), and the methionine malabsorption syndrome (or "oasthouse urine disease"). They are characterized by poor absorption of the amino acids tryptophan and methionine, respectively, from the small intestine.

NEPHROSCLEROSIS

Nephrosclerosis is a hardening of the walls of the small arteries and arterioles of the kidney. This condition is caused by hypertension. Hypertension can be present in a person for 20 to 30 years without evidence of kidney involvement. Such persons usually die of other effects of hypertension, such as congestion of blood in the heart, hardening of the heart tissue, or cerebral (brain) hemorrhage. If these maladies do not occur first, there is usually some eventual renal involvement. Nephrosclerosis is classified as either benign or malignant.

Benign nephrosclerosis is a gradual and prolonged deterioration of the renal arteries. First the inner layer of the walls of smaller vessels thickens, and gradually this thickening spreads to the whole wall, sometimes closing the central channel of the vessel. Fat then becomes deposited in the degenerated wall tissue. The larger arteries gain an excess of elastic tissue, which may block their channels. Both of these conditions cause the blood supply to the vital kidney areas to be blocked, and tissue deterioration ensues.

In malignant nephrosclerosis a similar process occurs but at a much faster rate. The disease may develop so rapidly that there is little time for gross kidney changes to occur. The surface of the kidney, however, is nearly always covered with large red blotches at points where bleeding has occurred. In the malignant disease the arteriole walls thicken and may be closed off by rapid cell growth. The nuclei of these cells die, and the elastic fibres disappear. With the loss of the elastic fibres, the walls of the vessels become much more fragile and easily distended. Severe ruptures and hemorrhages are frequent. The arterioles often suffer spasms that can force blood through lesions in the vessel walls. The tissues become swollen as a result. Malignant nephrosclerosis is accompanied by severe headache, confusion, blurred vision, nausea, and vomiting—all of which are caused by a drastic increase in blood pressure. Unless prompt treatment can relieve the increased blood pressure, tissue changes in the heart, culminating in heart failure, or in the brain, leading to seizures and coma, may occur.

The symptoms of nephrosclerosis include impaired vision, blood in the urine, loss of weight, and the accumulation of urea and other nitrogenous waste products in the blood (uremia). Treatment includes the administration of antihypertensive drugs, elimination of infection and of any obstruction, and other measures for relief of chronic renal failure.

Nephrotic Syndrome

Nephrotic syndrome, or nephrosis, is a group of signs of kidney malfunction, including a low level of albumin and a high level of lipids in the blood, proteins in the urine, and the accumulation of fluid in the tissues. Nephrotic syndrome typically results in the loss of more than 3.5 grams (0.12 ounces) of proteins per day. It may result from streptococcal infection, lupus erythematosus, renal vein thrombosis, or heavy-metal poisoning.

The nephrotic syndrome occurs usually in young children or young adults. Persons affected may lack appetite and experience irritability, vomiting, and diarrhea. High levels of fluids in the tissues can cause a 50 percent increase in body weight. In children the syndrome includes gross swelling of the face, while in adults the legs are most frequently afflicted. Low blood pressure and low plasma volume from lack of serum proteins occasionally cause severe vascular collapse. Protein malnutrition also leads to muscle wasting and growth retardation, especially in children. In treatment, attention is given to alleviation of the underlying disease and to elimination of the tissue fluids by increasing urine output.

Renal Cyst

A cyst is an enclosed sac or pouch that usually contains liquid or semisolid material. Several different types of cysts develop in the kidneys. Solitary cysts contain liquids and may be partially filled with blood. They vary widely in size. Some are present at birth, and others are caused by tubular obstructions. If sufficiently large, they can cause backaches and a dragging sensation. In kidney vascular diseases numerous small cysts may be formed by the dilatation of blood vessels. Obstruction of the lymphatic vessels leading to the kidney may result in cysts. These are generally small and relatively harmless except when they exert pressure upon a nearby blood vessel. Tapeworms may cause cysts in the kidneys. Symptoms include pain, difficulty in urination, blood in the urine, and the excretion of tapeworm eggs and segments in the urine. Usually, because of the possibility of a tumour, cysts require surgical exploration and removal.

Polycystic disease is a congenital defect in which one or both of the kidneys have numerous large cysts. In medullary cystic diseases, also thought to be congenital in origin, cysts form in the small collecting tubules that transport urine from the nephrons, the urine-producing units of the kidney. The disease generally does not have warning symptoms, but affected persons become anemic and have low salt concentrations and high levels of nitrogenous substances in the bloodstream. The kidneys shrink, have a granular surface, show many small cysts, and have large areas of scar tissue. The most common victims are older children and young adults.

RENAL OSTEODYSTROPHY

Renal osteodystrophy (or renal rickets) is a chronic, probably hereditary disorder characterized by kidney dysfunction, bone-mineral loss and rickets-type deformities, calcifications in abnormal places, and overactivity of the parathyroid glands. Loss of calcium and retention of phosphorus occur because of the malfunctioning kidneys. This induces an overproduction of parathormone, which results in the demineralization of well-formed bones and an inability to calcify newly developing bone. The bone abnormalities develop more slowly than kidney insufficiency. If the latter is severe, death may occur in childhood before the skeletal abnormalities become apparent. If the kidney insufficiency is not total, it may cause dwarfing and frequent fractures in children. Adults experience gradual softening and bowing of bones. Secondary hyperparathyroidism, a type of renal osteodystrophy, may be an acquired disease found in individuals with chronic renal failure. Although the effect of acquired disease on bone metabolism is more limited than that of hereditary renal osteodystrophy, because of its onset late in life, it causes similar changes in calcium and phosphorus metabolism and bone demineralization over time.

Treatment of renal osteodystrophy depends on the state of chemical balance of the patient. Kidney transplant has been successful in some cases involving severe kidney dysfunction, and removal of the malfunctioning parathyroids is sometimes effective in controlling symptoms.

UREMIA

The term *uremia* describes the toxic effects of abnormally high concentrations of nitrogenous substances in the blood as a result of the kidney's failure to expel these waste products by way of the urine. The end products of protein metabolism accumulate in the blood but are normally filtered out when the blood passes through the kidneys. Uremia can result from any disorder that impairs the functioning of the kidneys or that hinders the excretion of urine from the body.

The symptoms of uremia are diverse. Fatigue, lassitude, and a loss of mental concentration are among the first signs. The patient may experience persistent itching sensations, along with muscle twitching or other involuntary movements. The skin becomes dry, flaky, and turns yellowish to tan. The mouth has a dry metallic taste, and the breath has a distinct ammonialike odour. Loss of appetite progresses to nausea and vomiting, and episodes of diarrhea and constipation are common. In the more serious stages of uremia, the buildup of waste products in the bloodstream and tissues causes a wide-ranging derangement of the nervous, cardiovascular, and respiratory systems and can lead to hypertension, convulsions, heart failure, and death.

The chief cause of uremia is damage to the kidneys, whether because of Bright disease, hypertension (high blood pressure), diabetes mellitus, or some other disorder that impairs kidney function. Blockages of the flow of urine due to urinary stones or, in males, enlarged prostate glands can also cause uremia. The treatment of uremia rests on the identification and treatment of the disorder that is the underlying cause. Patients whose kidneys are diseased and who are waiting for kidney transplants often suffer varying degrees of uremia. In these cases uremia, along with other syndromes due to renal insufficiency, is best treated by dialysis—the artificial filtering of the blood by a machine outside the body.

MALIGNANT DISEASES OF THE RENAL SYSTEM

Malignant, or cancerous, tumours are distinguished from benign tumours by their abnormal growth rates and by the abnormal shapes, sizes, and functioning of their cells. In addition, whereas a benign tumour remains localized, confined to its site of origin, a malignant tumour spreads from its site of origin into nearby tissues or lymph nodes, or eventually to more distant sites via the blood or lymphatic system. In the case of the renal system, examples of malignant diseases include bladder cancer, nephroblastoma, and renal cell carcinoma.

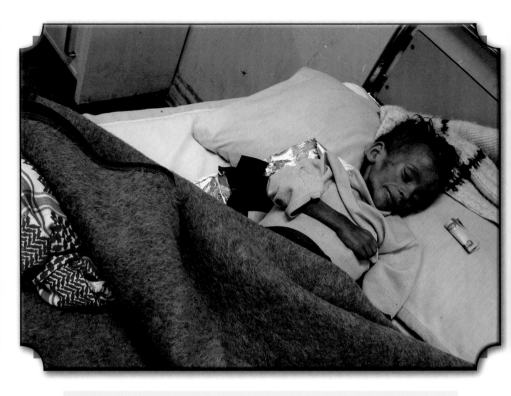

A young child with kidney cancer in Baghdad, Iraq. Nikos Pilos/Getty Images

BLADDER CANCER

Bladder cancer is a disease characterized by the growth of malignant cells within the urinary bladder, the organ responsible for storing urine prior to elimination. Bladder cancer can also be associated with cancers of the kidneys, ureters, or urethra.

Causes and Symptoms

Over 90 percent of bladder cancers are transitional cell carcinomas, or cancers of the cells lining the bladder, ureters, and urethra. The exact causes are largely unknown, but both genetic and environmental factors are responsible. In the United States bladder cancer is three times as likely to affect men as women, and whites are twice as likely to be affected as blacks. The most significant risk factor associated with bladder cancer is smoking—carcinogens (cancer-causing agents) are absorbed through the lungs into the bloodstream, where they are filtered out by the kidneys and enter the urinary tract. An environmental risk is presented by a class of organic chemicals called arylamines. People who work in the leather, rubber, printing, and textiles industries or with large quantities of paint are often exposed to these chemicals and should exercise caution in their use.

As with many cancers, advanced age is a risk factor, and most bladder cancers are diagnosed after the age of 60. Chronic bladder inflammation, such as that caused by recurrent bladder infections, is a risk factor, as are rare, inherited birth defects related to the development of the bladder.

The symptoms of bladder cancer are nearly identical to those of urinary tract infections and other diseases of the urogenital system. These symptoms include blood in the urine, difficulty urinating, excessive urination, or, more rarely, painful urination.

Diagnosis

In cases of suspected cancer, a urine sample or bladder washing is examined for the presence of abnormal cells, and the bladder can be examined visually, using a flexible tube called a cystoscope. The cystoscope is also used to take biopsy samples from the bladder or urethra for laboratory analysis. An X-ray imaging procedure called intravenous pyelography, in which an injectable dye travels into the urinary tract and enhances X-ray image contrast, may also be used. Abnormalities seen on the film may indicate the presence of cancer. In addition, laboratory tests can detect specific chemical markers that indicate cancer.

In order to determine the degree of metastasis, or spread of the cancer, several imaging methods may be used, such as traditional X-rays, CT scans, or magnetic resonance imaging (MRI). These procedures generate diagnostic pictures of different parts of the body and are used to detect abnormalities such as cancerous tissues.

Once bladder cancer has been diagnosed, its stage is then determined to indicate how far the cancer has progressed. Stage 0 bladder cancer, also called carcinoma in situ, is localized to the inner layer of the urinary bladder. Stage I cancers have spread into the connective tissue beneath the lining, and stage II cancers have progressed into the underlying muscle layer. Stage III bladder cancer has spread completely through the bladder wall and perhaps to nearby reproductive organs such as the uterus or prostate. Stage IV cancer extends to the abdominal wall and has usually spread to nearby lymph nodes. It may also have spread to other organs such as the lungs, liver, stomach, or bone.

When detected early, bladder cancers have a very high five-year survival rate, but the rate is only about 50 percent for those with local metastases. Bladder cancers that are detected late and have spread to distant regions of the body have a very low five-year survival rate.

Treatment and Prevention

Like most cancers, bladder cancer can be treated with surgery, radiation, or chemotherapy. Surgery is often the first method of treatment. When detected early, small regions of cancerous tissue may be surgically removed through the urethra, using a cystoscope in a procedure called transurethral resection. If the cancer has spread to a large region of the bladder, a cystectomy, or removal of bladder tissue, is necessary. In a partial cystectomy, only a portion of the bladder is removed and the remaining portion repaired. More invasive cancers require a radical cystectomy, or removal of the entire bladder. In men radical cystectomy usually includes removal of the prostate gland and seminal vesicles, and in women the ovaries, fallopian tubes, and uterus are usually removed.

Complete removal of the bladder requires an alternative method of storing urine. This is accomplished with a urostomy, in which a portion of the small intestine is removed and restructured to form a substitute for the bladder. Urine from the substitute bladder is then emptied into an external bag that is manually emptied when full, or the urine is stored in the intestinal sac and emptied through a catheter in the abdominal wall. In some cases, the resected portion of small intestine may be attached directly to the urethra, which allows for near normal urinary function.

Bladder cancer may be treated with radiation, using either external beams or surgically implanted radioactive rods or pellets. Radiation is usually employed following surgery to destroy small amounts of remaining cancerous tissue. The side effects of radiation treatment may include vomiting, diarrhea, fatigue, or skin irritations resembling a sunburn.

Chemotherapy may also be indicated for treatment of bladder cancers. If the cancer remains localized to the bladder, chemotherapeutic agents may be administered directly through a urinary catheter, which greatly reduces side effects by limiting exposure of other body tissues to the drugs. If the cancer has spread, systemic chemotherapy will be required, and several side effects resemble those of radiation therapy.

Bladder cancer may be treated through biological therapy, or immunotherapy, in which the body's own cells, chemicals, or other natural agents are used to help boost the natural immune response against the cancer. In some cases a special type of bacteria is injected directly into the bladder. The body's immune response is then targeted at the bacteria but also attacks the cancer.

Bladder cancer cannot be completely prevented, but risk of developing the disease can be greatly reduced by not smoking and by avoiding or reducing exposure to arylamines. People with uncontrollable risk factors such as advanced age or a personal history of bladder cancer should be aware of the early symptoms and see their physicians regularly.

Nephroblastoma

Nephroblastoma (also called embryoma, or Wilms' tumour) is a malignant tumour of the kidney occurring in early childhood. In 75 percent of the cases, the tumour grows before age five. About two-thirds of the instances are apparent by age two. The tumour grows rapidly and can approach the weight of the rest of the body. It rarely appears in adults. In its early stages the nephroblastoma causes no symptoms. Later, symptoms may indicate fever, distortion of the kidney mass, evidence of secondary tumours elsewhere in the body, abdominal and flank pain, weight loss, nausea, loss of appetite, and vomiting.

The tumour begins in the outer (cortical) tissue of the kidney. At first it is surrounded by a dense fibrous capsule. It is usually a grayish-white, soft mass. The tumour tends to destroy the whole kidney and spreads to neighbouring organs. It often causes secondary tumours (metastases) in the lungs, liver, brain, and bones.

The usual treatment of a nephroblastoma, if diagnosis is early enough, is a course of radiation before an operation, removal of the mass by surgery, and postoperative irradiation. Sometimes chemicals are given to slow the cell growth.

Renal Cell Carcinoma

Renal cell carcinoma is a disease arising from malignant epithelial cells in the kidneys. Renal cell carcinoma is responsible for about 85 percent of kidney cancers in adults.

Causes and Symptoms

Renal cell carcinoma appears to be caused by both genetic and environmental factors. Mutations in chromosome 3 have received special attention as an underlying cause. Men are twice as likely as women to develop this cancer, and the majority of cases are diagnosed in people between 50 and 70 years old. Smoking is believed to double the risk of developing renal cell carcinoma. Exposure to asbestos and cadmium are also suspected risk factors. Two rare disorders, tuberous sclerosis and von Hippel-Lindau syndrome, are often associated with renal cell cancers. Other risk factors include a family history of kidney cancer, long-term kidney dialysis, and obesity.

As with many cancers, the symptoms of renal cell carcinoma are often associated with other disorders. Symptoms include blood in the urine, unexplained pain in the side or lower back, anemia, fever, and unexplained weight loss. Because kidney cancer may affect the ability of the kidneys to regulate fluid levels in the body, high blood pressure or swelling of the feet or ankles may also occur.

Diagnosis

If cancer is suspected, a thorough examination is conducted to confirm its presence. Diagnosis is routinely made by means of multiple imaging techniques, including standard X-rays, CT scans, MRI, and ultrasound. A dye may be injected into a vein and allowed to travel to the kidney in order to improve X-ray contrast. Although no laboratory test exists for diagnosing renal cell carcinoma, urinalysis may reveal blood in the urine, and a blood test may reveal anemia, elevated liver enzymes, or elevated calcium levels. Results of these tests may indicate the possibility of kidney cancer and thus allow early diagnosis and treatment.

Once renal cell cancer has been diagnosed, its stage is then determined to indicate how far the cancer has progressed. Stage I tumours are less than 7 cm (about 2¾ inches) and are confined to the kidney, whereas stage II tumours are larger than 7 cm. Stage III tumours have spread to the tissues surrounding the kidney, the adjacent adrenal gland, the major blood vessels of the kidney, or nearby lymph nodes. Stage IV cancers have spread to other areas of the body such as the liver, lungs, colon, pancreas, or bone.

The average five-year survival rate for all stages of renal cell carcinoma combined is less than 50 percent, as approximately one-third of renal cell carcinomas have already metastasized by the time of diagnosis. The five-year survival rate is very low once the cancer has spread to distant organs. Survival is considerably higher when the cancer is detected early. Many of these patients often go on to live long, healthy lives.

Treatment and Prevention

Unlike many other cancers, renal cell carcinoma generally does not respond well to chemotherapy or radiation.

Therefore, surgery is usually necessary. A nephrectomy, or removal of kidney tissue, is the most common procedure. Partial nephrectomy removes only a portion of the kidney, while the more common radical nephrectomy removes an entire kidney plus the adrenal gland. Often local lymph nodes are also removed.

Although chemotherapy and radiation treatments are generally not effective in curing renal cell carcinoma, they may be used in conjunction with surgery or in cases where surgery is not indicated owing to generally poor health. Biological therapies involving the immune system are also used to combat kidney cancer.

Besides the elimination of risk factors, little is known about how to prevent kidney cancer. Patients with chronic kidney failure who are on dialysis, however, should receive periodic X-rays to look for the early signs of renal cell carcinoma.

CLEAR CELL RENAL CELL CARCINOMA

Clear cell renal cell carcinoma is the most common type of renal cell carcinoma, accounting for roughly 65 percent of cases. It is named for the clear or pale yellow appearance of the cells when viewed under a light microscope.

Most clear cell renal cell carcinomas appear in persons past age 40, with peak incidence around the sixth or seventh decade. They tend to arise in persons with vascular disorders of the kidneys. Because they are in close proximity to the bloodstream, they frequently send secondary tumours to other organs of the body such as the lungs, liver, brain, and bone tissue.

The carcinoma forms a large rounded mass in one or both of the kidneys. It is chiefly yellow in colour because of the large amount of lipid (fat) substances present. There are also reddened areas, where blood vessels have bled, and cysts containing watery fluids. The body of the tumour generally shows numerous large blood vessels, the walls of which are composed of tumour cells.

Clear cell renal cell carcinomas are frequently not recognized until they manifest themselves in other parts of the body. Painless bleeding into the urine may occur early in the disease but is usually disregarded by the person afflicted. Pain is uncommon until late in the development of the disease. The tumour causes deformity in one or more of the cavities in the kidney at an early stage. If tumours are suspected, a specialized X-ray will show these distortions.

Clear cell renal cell carcinoma may spontaneously regress. After a tumour has been surgically removed there may be no recurrence, or there may be a recurrence as much as 20 years later.

CHAPTER 6

Evaluation and Treatment of Renal Diseases and Disorders

The choice of therapy for diseases and disorders of the renal system depends on the evaluation of disease, which is a central part of diagnosis. Diagnosis is based largely on the characteristic symptoms expressed by the diseased renal tissue and on abnormalities in urine composition. Such abnormalities often are readily detected by quantitative tests for renal function, including tests for creatinine clearance and inulin clearance.

The identification of factors such as the presence of infectious agents, which may be detected through urinalysis, is another essential element of evaluation that guides therapeutic approaches to disease control. Other important methods of evaluation include the visual examination of tissues with techniques such as urography and ultrasound. Renal function tests and visual evaluations are used to inform decisions concerning whether or when advanced treatments, such as dialysis or kidney transplant, must be considered.

THE STUDY OF RENAL FUNCTION

The study of kidney function and the treatment of kidney disease forms the basis of the branch of medicine known as nephrology. The first scientific observations of the kidney were made by Italian physicians Lorenzo Bellini and Marcello Malpighi in the middle of the 17th century, but true physiological understanding of the kidney began with German physiologist Carl Ludwig's 1844 hypothesis that blood pressure forces waste fluids out of the renal capillaries into the nephrons of the kidney. In 1899 British physiologist Ernest Starling further explained the function of the kidney by proposing that osmotic pressures helped to concentrate the urine there. This theory was confirmed by American physiologist Alfred N. Richards in the 1920s.

Clinical nephrology, the treatment of kidney diseases, emerged from the disciplines of urology and cardiology as more knowledge was gained about kidney functions. Despite increased information, however, there was little that could be done to treat patients with severe kidney disease before the 1950s. The first artificial kidney capable of removing blood impurities by hemodialysis was developed during World War II but could be used only for temporary, reversible renal collapse. It was not until American physician Belding Scribner in 1960 demonstrated the usefulness of the permanent Teflon arteriovenous shunt that repeated hemodialysis for chronic renal disease became feasible. Instantly, the outlook for patients with irreversible

Ernest H. Starling. Time & Life Pictures/Getty Images

kidney disease changed from certain death to 90-percent survival. The long-range prospects for these patients was further enhanced by the development of kidney transplants, first successfully performed in 1954 on identical twins. Transplants from cadavers, which were more generally applicable, also began in the 1950s. In the 1960s, the clinical use of kidney transplants increased, largely as a result of the development of immunosuppressive agents that reduce the risk of transplant rejection.

Subsequent advances in the diagnosis and treatment of kidney diseases paralleled advances in fields such as genetics and regenerative medicine. Indeed, the identification and characterization of genetic mutations that underlie certain hereditary kidney diseases has resulted in improved diagnosis and treatment of these conditions. Likewise, progress in regenerative medicine—the application of treatments developed to replace tissues damaged by injury or disease—has led to the creation and successful transplantation of synthetic bladders and ureters.

EVALUATING RENAL FUNCTION

Certain diagnostic techniques with respect to urine composition and renal function are important factors in determining the degree of renal disease and the appropriate medical and surgical treatment. Through a variety of laboratory tests, physicians can assess renal blood flow and determine whether the nephrons are functioning properly and even whether a specific protein or amino acid is excreted in excess. The results of such analyses enable physicians to make accurate diagnoses and formulate effective treatment regimens for renal disease.

QUANTITATIVE TESTS

Important quantitative tests of renal function include those of glomerular filtration rate, renal clearance, and renal blood flow. Tests are also made to estimate maximal tubular activity, tubular mass, and tubular function. Radiological and other imaging methods are useful non-invasive diagnostic techniques, and renal biopsy is valuable in detecting pathological changes that affect the kidneys.

In both clinical and experimental studies one of the most fundamental measures of renal function is that of the glomerular filtration rate (GFR). The GFR is calculated by measuring the specific clearance from the body of a substance believed to be excreted solely by glomerular filtration. The renal clearance of any substance is the volume of plasma containing that amount of the substance that is removed by the kidney in unit time (e.g., in one minute). Clearance, or the volume of plasma cleared, is an artificial concept since no portion of the plasma is ever really cleared in this fashion.

It was soon realized, however, that if a substance could be found that was freely filtered by the glomeruli and was neither reabsorbed, metabolized, nor secreted by the renal tubules, its clearance would equal the GFR. This is so in these circumstances because the amount of such a substance excreted in the urine in one minute would equal the amount that has been filtered at the glomeruli in the same time. If the concentration of the substance in the plasma (which is the same as that in the glomerular filtrate) is known, the clearance volume must represent the volume of glomerular filtrate.

The first substance identified to be excreted in this way was the polysaccharide inulin (molecular weight about

5,000), which is extracted from the roots of dahlias. Although inulin is not naturally found in human plasma it is nontoxic and can be injected or infused into the bloodstream. Its concentration also can be measured readily and accurately.

Clearance value is not the same as excretion rate. The clearance of inulin and some other compounds is not altered by raising its plasma concentration, because the amount of urine completely cleared of the agent remains the same. But the excretion rate equals total quantity excreted per millilitre of filtrate per minute, and this value is directly proportional to its plasma concentration.

Substances, such as urea, whose clearance is less than the GFR must be reabsorbed by the renal tubules, while substances whose clearance is greater than the GFR must be secreted by the renal tubules. Since the discovery of inulin, researchers have identified a small number of other substances that are excreted by the kidney in a similar fashion and that have similar clearance values. These include vitamin B_{12}, circulating free in plasma and unbound to protein, and sodium ferrocyanide.

The clearance of creatinine was used as a measure of renal function before inulin was discovered; because this substance is found naturally in plasma, creatinine clearance is still widely used as an approximate measure of the GFR. Creatinine is produced in the body at virtually a constant rate, and its concentration in the blood changes little. Accordingly, creatinine clearance is usually measured over a period of 24 hours. There is evidence that in humans creatinine is secreted into the urine by renal tubules as well. However, the amount is small and constant and has little effect on the measure of the GFR.

The concept of clearance is also useful in the measurement of renal blood flow. Para-aminohippuric acid (PAH), when introduced into the bloodstream and kept at relatively low plasma concentrations, is rapidly excreted into the urine by both glomerular filtration and tubular secretion. Sampling of blood from the renal vein reveals that 90 percent of PAH is removed by a single circulation of blood through the kidneys. This high degree of PAH extraction by the kidney at a single circulation implies that the clearance of PAH is approximately the same as renal plasma flow (RPF). The 10 percent of PAH that remains in renal venous blood is conveyed in blood that perfuses either nonsecretory tissue, such as fibrous tissue or fat, or parts of the tubule that do not themselves secrete PAH. In practice this small remaining percentage is usually ignored, and the clearance of PAH is referred to as the effective renal plasma flow. In humans PAH clearance is about 600 ml (20.3 fluid ounces) per minute, and thus true renal plasma flow is about 700 ml (23.7 fluid ounces) per minute.

Estimation of the GFR and RPF allows the proportion of available plasma perfusing the kidney that is filtered by the glomerulus to be calculated. This is called the filtration fraction and on average in healthy individuals is 125/600, or about 20 percent. Thus about one-fifth of plasma entering the glomeruli leaves as filtrate, the remaining four-fifths continuing into the efferent glomerular arterioles. This fraction changes in a number of clinical disorders, notably hypertension.

Reference has already been made to the fact that the renal tubules possess a limited capacity to perform certain of their functions. This is the case, for example, in their ability to concentrate and dilute urine and to achieve a gradient of hydrogen ions between urine and blood. Concentrating power can be tested by depriving the individual of water for up to 24 hours, or, more simply, by introducing a synthetic analogue of vasopressin into each nostril. The water deprivation test assesses the individual's capacity to produce vasopressin and the sensitivity of the renal concentrating mechanism to circulating vasopressin. The use of an analogue of vasopressin assesses only the sensitivity of the renal tubules to the hormone.

The limits of renal ability to excrete acid and establish a gradient of the concentration of hydrogen ions between plasma and urine has been mentioned above. The power of acidification of urine is best estimated by measuring the pH of urine after the administration of ammonium chloride in divided doses over two or three days. Other specific functions that are tested include the individual's ability to conserve sodium, potassium, and magnesium. In general, these tests are carried out by administering diets that are deficient in these electrolytes and then estimating the minimum rate of excretion after several days.

Kidney Function Test

A kidney function test is any clinical and laboratory procedure designed to evaluate various aspects of renal capacity and efficiency and to aid in the diagnosis of kidney disorders. Such tests can be divided into several categories, which include (1) concentration and dilution tests, whereby the specific gravity of urine is determined at regular time intervals following water restriction or large water intake, to measure the capacity of the kidneys to conserve water, (2) clearance tests, which give an estimate of the filtration rate of the glomeruli, the principal filtering structures of the kidneys, and overall renal blood flow, (3) visual and physical examination of the urine, which usually includes the recording of its physical characteristics such as colour, total volume, and specific gravity, as well as checking for the abnormal presence of pus, hyaline casts (precipitation of pure protein from the kidney tubules), and red and white blood cells. Proteinuria, the presence of protein in the urine, is often the first abnormal finding indicative of kidney disease, (4) determination of the concentration of various substances in the urine, notably glucose, amino acids, phosphate, sodium, and potassium, to help detect possible impairment of the specific kidney mechanisms normally involved with their reabsorption.

Creatinine Clearance

Creatinine clearance is a clinical measurement used to estimate renal function, specifically the filtration rate of the glomeruli. Creatinine is a chemical end product of creatine metabolism that is removed, or cleared, from blood plasma by glomeruli and is excreted in the urine. The creatinine clearance value is determined by measuring the concentration of endogenous creatinine (that which is produced by the body) in both plasma and urine; the reference value for men is 85–125 ml (2.9–4.2 fluid ounces) per minute and that for women is 75–115 ml (2.5–3.9 fluid ounces) per minute. A low or decreased creatinine clearance level may indicate conditions such as glomerulonephritis, ureteral obstruction, or pyelonephritis.

Creatinine clearance is a slightly less accurate measure of the glomerular filtration rate than inulin clearance because, unlike inulin, a small amount of creatinine is reabsorbed by the kidney and is not excreted in the urine, thereby being lost to measurement. Difficulties involved in carrying out the inulin clearance procedure, however, render creatinine clearance the more practical clinical measurement with which to assess renal function.

Inulin Clearance

Inulin clearance is a procedure by which the filtering capacity of the glomeruli is determined by measuring the rate at which inulin, the test substance, is cleared from blood plasma. Inulin is the most accurate substance to measure because it is a small, inert polysaccharide molecule that readily passes through the glomeruli into the urine without being reabsorbed by the renal tubules. The steps involved in this measurement, however, are quite involved. Consequently, inulin is seldom used in clinical testing, although it is used in research.

Phenolsulfonphthalein Test

The phenolsulfonphthalein test, or PSP test, is a clinical procedure for the estimation of overall blood flow through the kidney. It is used infrequently, having been replaced in large part by other diagnostic tests. In a PSP test, a specific dose of the PSP dye is injected intravenously, and its recovery in the urine is measured at successive 15-, 30-, 60-, and 120-minute intervals. The kidney secretes 80 percent of the PSP dye, the liver the remaining 20 percent. The recovery value at 15 minutes after injection (normally about 25–35 percent) is the most significant diagnostically, since even a damaged kidney may be able to remove the PSP dye from circulation given a longer time to do so. PSP excretion is decreased in most chronic kidney diseases and may be increased in some liver disorders.

RENAL BIOPSY

The visual, usually microscopic, examination of a specimen of kidney tissue removed from a living patient (renal biopsy) is the only investigative method that yields exact histological data on renal structure. The material for examination is usually obtained by inserting a special needle through the skin of the back into the kidney substance and withdrawing a fragment of tissue. A general anesthetic is not usually required, the procedure occupying only a few minutes. Renal biopsy has been valuable in clarifying several renal disorders, notably those affecting the glomeruli, and in revealing their prognosis and natural course. The major, potentially serious complication of biopsy is excessive bleeding, but this is rare. The procedure is not justified, however, if the patient possesses only one kidney or suffers from a bleeding disorder or from severe, uncontrolled high blood pressure.

EVALUATION OF URINARY FUNCTION

The evaluation of urinary function specifically is the focus of the medical specialty known as urology. Urology involves the diagnosis and treatment of diseases and disorders of the urinary tract and of the male reproductive organs.

The modern specialty derives directly from the medieval lithologists, who were itinerant healers specializing in the surgical removal of bladder stones. In 1588 the Spanish surgeon Francisco Diaz wrote the first treatises on diseases of the bladder, kidneys, and urethra. He is generally regarded as the founder of modern urology.

Most modern urologic procedures developed during the 19th century. At that time flexible catheters were developed for examining and draining the bladder, and in 1877 the German urologist Max Nitze developed the cystoscope. The cystoscope is a tubelike viewing instrument equipped with an electric light on its end. By introducing the instrument through the urethra, the urologist is able to view the interior of the bladder. The first decades of the early 20th century witnessed the introduction of various X-ray techniques that have proved extremely useful in diagnosing disorders of the urinary tract. Urologic surgery was largely confined to the removal of bladder stones until the German surgeon Gustav Simon in 1869 demonstrated that human patients could survive the removal of one kidney, provided the remaining kidney was healthy.

Most of the modern urologist's patients are male, for two reasons: (1) the urinary tract in females may be treated by gynecologists, and (2) much of the urologist's work has to do with the prostate gland, which encircles the male urethra close to the juncture between the urethra and the bladder. The prostate gland is often the site of cancer. Even more frequently, it enlarges in middle or old age and encroaches on the urethra, causing partial or complete obstruction of the flow of urine. The urologist treats prostate enlargement either by totally excising the prostate or by reaming a wider passageway through it. Urologists may also operate to remove stones that have formed in the urinary tract, and they may perform operations to remove cancers of the kidneys, bladder, and testicles.

UROSCOPY AND URINALYSIS

Uroscopy is a medical examination of the urine that is used to facilitate the diagnosis of a disease or disorder. Examining the urine is one of the oldest forms of diagnostic testing, extending back to the days of the ancient Greek physician Hippocrates. Physicians observed the urine to diagnose all forms of illness because direct examination of a patient, or at least disrobing the patient, was socially unacceptable. Until the mid-19th century, uroscopy remained a common method for diagnosing illness. The colour of the urine, as well as cloudiness, precipitates, and particles in the urine, was believed to indicate the cause of the disorder.

Today urinalysis, which is the laboratory examination of a sample of urine to obtain clinical information, is the most commonly performed test in the physician's office. It consists of (1) a gross examination, in which the colour, the turbidity, and the specific gravity of the urine are assessed; (2) the use of a dipstick (a plastic strip containing reagent pads) to test for bilirubin, blood, glucose, ketones, leukocyte esterase, nitrite, pH, protein, and urobilinogen; and (3) a microscopic examination of a centrifuged specimen to detect erythrocytes (red blood cells) or leukocytes (white blood cells), casts, crystals, and bacteria. The urine is collected by using a "clean-catch" technique to eliminate contamination with bacteria from skin or vaginal secretions.

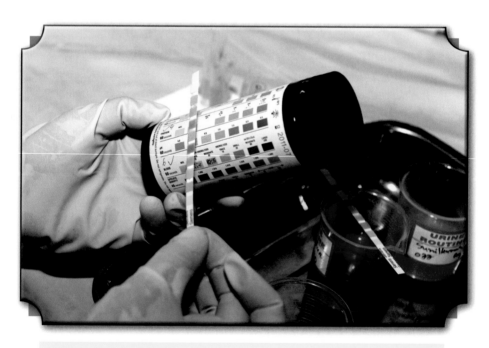

An Indian pathologist examines a urine sample. Sam Panthaky/AFP/ Getty Images

Dipstick tests are available that contain from 2 to 10 different tests. The test for glucose, which likely indicates diabetes mellitus, and the test for protein, which indicates kidney disease, tumours of the urinary tract, or hypertensive disorders of pregnancy, are two of the most important assays available.

The microscopic examination is the most valuable urinalysis test. It will show a variety of cells that are normally shed from the urinary tract. Usually up to five white blood cells per high-power field (HPF) are present. However, the presence of more than 10 white blood cells per HPF indicates a urinary tract infection. Red blood cells in the urine sediment can be indicative of urinary tract inflammation and can also be a sign of a malignant tumour of the kidney, the bladder, or the urinary tract. A count of more than two red blood cells per HPF is abnormal, although in women this is often due to vaginal contamination from menstruation.

The identification of red blood cells in the urine (hematuria) always demands follow-up to determine the cause and to rule out the presence of a neoplasm (tumour). Cylindrically shaped urinary casts, shed from the kidney's tubules, consist of protein mixed with cells or other materials and may indicate renal disease if present in large numbers. Various crystals also are found in the urinary sediment, but these are generally of little clinical significance. Occasionally, the presence of specific crystals may help confirm a diagnosis. For example, uric acid crystals in the urine may be associated with gout.

RADIOLOGICAL AND OTHER IMAGING INVESTIGATIONS

Imaging techniques are used to determine the anatomical site, configuration, and level of functioning of the kidneys, pelvis, and ureters. A plain X-ray nearly always precedes any other more elaborate investigation, so that the size, outline, and position of the two kidneys, as well as information about the presence or absence of calcium-containing renal stones or zones of calcification can be ascertained.

Urography is the X-ray examination of any part of the urinary tract after introduction of a radiopaque substance (often an organic iodine derivative) that casts an X-ray shadow. This contrast fluid, which passes quickly into the urine, may be taken orally or injected intravenously. It may also be injected directly into the area being examined. Tumours, tuberculous abscesses, kidney stones, and obstruction by prostatic enlargement may be detected by this method. Specific types of urography include

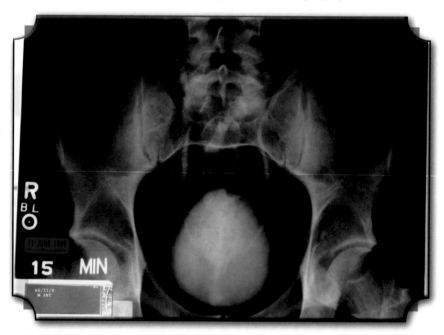

An X-ray contrast image of the kidneys and bladder. ©www/istockphoto.com/spxChrome

pyelography (examination of the kidney and ureter) and cystography (examination of the bladder). Motion-picture "voiding cystograms" provide evidence of gross reflux of urine into the ureters and pelvis of the kidney during voiding.

Excretion urography is another method used to examine the kidneys visually, though this radiological method is giving way to noninvasive imaging methods such as ultrasound and magnetic resonance imaging (MRI). Excretion urography can be used to provide information on both the structure and the function of the renal system. In this test the kidneys are observed in X-rays after intravenous injection of a radiopaque compound that is excreted largely by glomerular filtration within one hour of the injection. A series of X-ray images (nephrograms) then indicates when the contrast substance first appears and reveals the increasing radiographic density of the renal tissue. The X-rays also indicate the position, size, and presence of scarring or tumours in the organs and provide an approximate comparison of function in the two kidneys. Finally the dye collects in the bladder, revealing any rupture or tumour in this organ.

A micturating cystogram (voiding cystourethrogram [VCUG]) involves the injection of contrast substance into the bladder and is of importance in the investigation of urinary tract infection in childhood. It may show the reflux of urine from the bladder upward into the ureters or kidneys on micturition. Because of the risk of radiation to the gonads this test should be conducted only on certain patients.

A radioactive renogram involves the injection of radioactive compounds that are concentrated and excreted by the kidney. The radiation can be detected by placing gamma scintillation counters externally over the kidneys at the back. The counts, transcribed on moving graph paper, yield characteristic time curves for normal and disordered function.

A picture of renal circulation can be obtained by introducing a radiopaque substance into the renal arteries via a catheter tube placed through a more peripheral artery in the groin area. The contrast material yields a renal angiogram, showing the renal vascular tree. The technique is especially valuable in demonstrating the presence of localized narrowing or obstructions in the circulation or of localized dilatations (aneurysms). Tumours, which tend to be well vascularized, are also distinguishable from cysts, which are not well supplied with blood. Balloon-tipped catheters can be used to stop active bleeding or to introduce a supportive stent, which is permanently placed inside an artery to stabilize a weakened vessel or to keep a narrowed vessel open.

Ultrasound and MRI have the advantage of being noninvasive and thus pose little risk to the patient. They are useful in detecting tumours of the kidney or adjacent structures and in distinguishing tumours from cysts. Special contrast agents (e.g., gadolinium) may be infused before a MRI examination to evaluate metabolic characteristics of tissues and to facilitate the examination of blood flow to a tumour. This may help to differentiate between benign and cancerous tumours. Ultrasound techniques are comparatively simple and have replaced other methods in detecting the presence of polycystic kidneys, as well as in providing initial screening evaluation of the kidney.

KIDNEY TRANSPLANT

Kidney transplant, also called renal transplant, is the replacement of a diseased or damaged kidney with a healthy one obtained either from a living relative or a recently deceased person. Kidney transplant is a treatment for persons who have chronic renal failure requiring dialysis.

Although kidney transplants were carried out in the late 1950s, clinically significant transplantation did not begin until around 1963, when the immunosuppressive drug azathioprine was developed to help counteract the rejection of the new organ by the body's immune system. Because a kidney from a related donor is less likely to be rejected by the body, transplants from living relatives are more successful than those from cadavers. Nevertheless, cadavers are today the most common source for transplants because of their greater availability and because they obviate the risk to living donors. The development of more effective immunosuppressive drugs such as cyclosporine has increased the success rates of both related donor and cadaver kidney transplants. Today, more than four-fifths of patients with transplanted kidneys will survive for more than five years.

Transplantation and Postoperative Care

Before transplantation, the immunologic characteristics of the recipient are carefully analyzed and a donor selected whose immunologic profile is matched as closely to the recipient's as possible. Traits used in determining a successful match include blood groups and tissue markers that enable the immune system to distinguish between the body's own tissues and foreign tissue. A transplant operation will be cancelled if the recipient has any infection, because of the risk that infection will spread, protected by immunosuppressive medication. Persons with chronic renal failure who also have active cancer are not considered candidates for kidney transplant, because immunosuppressive drugs may suppress the body's ability to contain the cancer.

The new kidney is implanted in the iliac fossa, a space in the groin area just below and to the side of the umbilicus. Usually a right kidney is placed in the left fossa and vice versa to aid in making new attachments between blood vessels. The renal artery and vein are connected to the iliac artery and vein, and the ureter from the new kidney is either connected to the existing ureter or attached directly to the bladder. Formerly both of the recipient's kidneys were removed. They are now left in place unless they are infected or are too large to permit the new organ to be implanted.

Following a kidney transplant, every effort is made to keep the patient from contact with bacteria that might cause infection. The patient is usually nursed in a separate room, and doctors and nurses entering the room take care to wear masks and wash their hands before touching him. The air of the room is purified by filtration. Close relatives are allowed to visit the patient, but they are required to take the same precautions.

Some degree of rejection, although treatable with medications, is fairly common, especially for cadaver kidneys. Some patients receive two or three kidneys before the body accepts one. Rejection may begin within minutes after the new organ is attached. Acute rejection, in which the tissues of the new kidney are injured by the immune system and the organ suddenly fails to function, can occur up to several years after operation but is most common in the first three months. Chronic rejection, in which deterioration of kidney function is more gradual, also may occur. Large doses of immunosuppressive drugs, along with drugs that retard the formation of blood clots, can halt acute rejection and save the transplant. If the medication does not help, the kidney is usually removed before infection or other complications set in.

Kidneys taken from living donors often begin to function immediately, while those from cadavers may take up to two weeks for tissues to adjust and become functional. The patient may be discharged from the hospital within a few weeks of the operation, but frequent return visits are necessary for medical examination and biochemical estimations of the blood constituents, to determine the state of function of the graft, and to make sure that the drugs are not causing side effects. If there are no complications from the transplant and no signs of rejection, the recipient can resume a virtually normal life within two months, although he or she must usually continue taking immunosuppressive drugs for several years. Because these drugs lower resistance to infection, however, other systemic complications may arise with time.

If the patient rejects the kidney or develops a serious infection, it may be necessary to remove the graft and stop administration of the immunosuppressive drugs. The patient must then return to regular maintenance treatment with dialysis but may receive a second or even a third graft.

DATA ON KIDNEY TRANSPLANT RESULTS

In kidney grafts involving identical twins, in which case rejection is not a problem, recipients have survived more than 25 years. A number of patients who have received kidneys from unrelated cadaver donors have survived more than 20 years, demonstrating that in some patients rejection can be controlled with standard immunosuppressive drugs. There has been a gradual improvement in the overall results of kidney transplants. The patient mortality has declined to around 5–10 percent per year, death usually being due to infection associated with immunosuppressive treatment, to complications of dialysis in patients whose kidneys have failed, or to other facets of kidney disease, such as high blood pressure and coronary artery disease.

Recipients also face an increased risk of developing malignant growths, particularly lymphomas (malignant diseases of the lymphatic system). One cause of this may be related to the effects of immunosuppressive treatment. Kidney-graft survival has improved since the introduction of the immunosuppressive agent cyclosporine (also called cyclosporin A), and many centres have achieved a one-year survival rate of 80–85 percent and a two-year rate of 70 percent for patients with a functioning kidney graft from an unrelated cadaver donor. One-year survival rates of 80 to 90 percent have been attained for kidney grafts between parent and child and more than 90 percent for grafts from well-matched sibling donors. As these statistics indicate, the patient who develops permanent kidney failure now has a reasonable chance of good treatment from a combination of dialysis and kidney transplantation. Those fortunate enough to receive a well-functioning kidney can expect complete rehabilitation.

DIALYSIS

Dialysis, or hemodialysis (also called renal, or kidney, dialysis), is the process of removing blood from a patient whose kidney functioning is faulty, purifying that blood by dialysis, and returning it to the patient's bloodstream. The artificial kidney, or hemodialyzer, is a machine that provides a means for removing certain undesirable substances from the blood or of adding needed components to it. By these processes the apparatus can control the acid–base balance of the blood and its content of water and dissolved materials. Another known function of the natural kidney—secretion of hormones that influence the blood pressure—cannot be duplicated. Modern dialyzers rely on two physicochemical principles, dialysis and ultrafiltration.

In dialysis two liquids separated by a porous membrane exchange those components that exist as particles small enough to diffuse through the pores. When the blood is brought into contact with one side of such a membrane, dissolved substances (including urea and inorganic salts) pass through into a sterile solution placed on the other side of the membrane. The red and white cells, platelets, and proteins cannot penetrate the membrane because the particles are too large. To prevent or limit the loss of diffusible substances required by the body, such as sugars, amino acids, and necessary amounts of salts, those compounds are added to the sterile solution. Thus their diffusion from the blood is offset by equal movement in the opposite direction. The lack of diffusible materials in the blood can be corrected by incorporating them in the solution, from which they enter the circulation.

Although water passes easily through the membrane, it is not removed by dialysis because its concentration in the blood is lower than in the solution; indeed, water tends to pass from the solution into the blood. The dilution of the blood that would result from this process is prevented by ultrafiltration, by which some of the water, along with some dissolved materials, is forced through the membrane by maintaining the blood at a higher pressure than the solution.

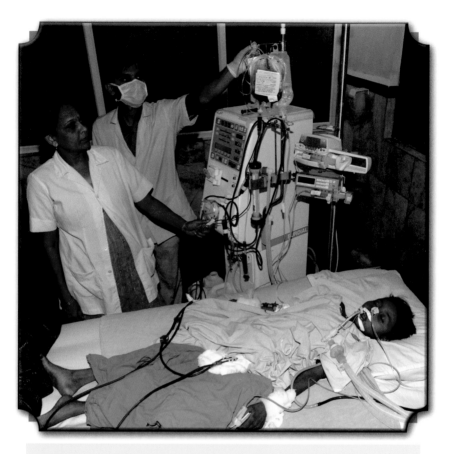

A child on a dialysis machine. Sam Panthaky/AFP/Getty Images

The membranes first used in dialysis were obtained from animals or prepared from collodion. Cellophane has been found to be more suitable, and tubes or sheets of it are used in many dialyzers. In the late 1960s hollow filaments of cellulosic or synthetic materials were introduced for dialysis. Bundles of such filaments provide a large membrane surface in a small volume, a combination advantageous in devising compact dialyzers.

Dialysis—which was first used to treat human patients in 1945—replaces or supplements the action of the kidneys in a person suffering from acute or chronic renal failure or from poisoning by diffusible substances, such as aspirin, bromides, or barbiturates. Blood is diverted from an artery, usually one in the wrist, into the dialyzer, where it flows—either by its own impetus or with the aid of a mechanical pump—along one surface of the membrane. Finally the blood passes through a trap that removes clots and bubbles and returns to a vein in the patient's forearm. In persons with chronic kidney failure, who require frequent dialysis, repeated surgical access to the blood vessels used in the treatments is obviated by provision of an external plastic shunt between them.

CONCLUSION

The confirmation in the early 20th century of osmotic pressure as the force behind the concentration of urine in the kidney drew attention to the complex physiology of this organ. Since then, the discovery of different mechanisms of transport across renal epithelial membranes and the characterization of membrane permeability in different regions of the nephron have contributed to significant advances in scientists' understanding of the kidney and renal system in both health and disease. Still, much remains to be discovered about this extraordinary system. For example, a complete understanding of the underlying mechanisms that mediate the autoregulatory control of blood through the capillaries in the glomerulus continues to elude scientists, despite decades of research.

Advances in biochemistry, genetics, and biotechnology have placed kidney and renal science at the forefront of medicine. Some of the most influential breakthroughs in renal medicine have come from progress in stem cell research and tissue engineering, both of which are central to the field of regenerative medicine. Tissue engineering, which integrates biological components, such as cells and growth factors, with engineering principles and synthetic materials, has provided scientists with the tools necessary to develop biological substitutes capable of replacing diseased or damaged tissue. In the case of the renal system, the generation and successful transplantation of urinary bladders and urethras has broadened therapeutic opportunities for complicated renal disorders.

GLOSSARY

afferent Conveying impulses toward the central nervous system.

angiotensin Either of two forms of a kinin of which one has marked vasoconstrictive action.

calyx A cuplike animal structure (such as the body wall of a crinoid or a division of the kidney pelvis).

catecholamine Any of various amines (such as epinephrine, norepinephrine, and dopamine) that function as hormones or neurotransmitters or both.

corticosteroid Any of various adrenal-cortex steroids (such as corticosterone , cortisone, and aldosterone) used medically, especially as anti-inflammatory agents.

diuresis An increased excretion of urine.

efferent Conveying nervous impulses to an effector , such as a muscle.

efflux Something given off in or as if in a stream.

glomerulus A tuft of capillaries at the point of origin of each vertebrate nephron that passes a protein-free filtrate to the surrounding Bowman's capsule.

homeostasis A relatively stable state of equilibrium between different but interdependent elements or groups.

incontinence The inability of the body to control the evacuative functions of urination or defecation.

innervate To supply with nerves.

kidney One of a pair of vertebrate organs situated in the body cavity near the spinal column that excrete waste products of metabolism.

lumen The cavity of a tubular organ or part.

micturate Urinate.

nephron A single excretory unit of the vertebrate kidney.

perfusion The act of forcing a fluid through (an organ or tissue), especially by way of the blood vessels.

peristaltic Relating to waves of involuntary contraction passing along the walls of a hollow muscular structure, forcing its contents onward.

pudendal Of or relating to the external genital organs of a human, especially of a woman.

renin A proteolytic enzyme of the kidney that plays a major role in the release of angiotensin.

serous Of, relating to, or resembling serum.

somatic Of, relating to, or affecting the body especially as distinguished from the germplasm or the psyche.

sphincter An annular muscle surrounding and able to contract or close a bodily opening.

tubule A slender elongated anatomical channel.

ureter A duct that carries urine away from a kidney to the bladder or cloaca.

urethra The canal that in most mammals carries off the urine from the bladder and in the male serves also as a passageway for semen.

vasoconstriction Narrowing of the lumen of blood vessels.

vasopressin A polypeptide hormone secreted by the posterior lobe of the pituitary gland or obtained synthetically that increases blood pressure and decreases urine flow; also known as antidiuretic hormone.

BIBLIOGRAPHY

Don W. Fawcett, William Bloom, and Elio Raviola, *A Textbook of Histology*, 12th ed. (1994), an illustrated text on histology and fine structure; Henry Gray, *Anatomy of the Human Body*, 30th American ed., edited by Carmine D. Clemente (1985), a treatise frequently revised over the past century and still regarded as one of the great anatomical texts; and Bruce M. Carlson, *Human Embryology and Developmental Biology*, 3rd ed. (2004), one of the leading textbooks on human embryology. Michael J. Field, David Harris, and Carol A. Pollock, *The Renal System* (2001), is a useful introductory textbook covering the basic science of the renal system.

The following works provide detailed and well-written surveys of the field of kidney function in a form suitable for medical students and for others with a good scientific grounding: E.J. Moran Campbell et al. (eds.), *Clinical Physiology*, 5th ed. (1984); and J.M. Forrester et al. (eds.), *A Companion to Medical Studies: Anatomy, Biochemistry, and Physiology*, 3rd ed. (1985).

Arthur Greenberg, *Primer on Kidney Diseases*, 4th ed. (2005), is a publication of the U.S. National Kidney Foundation that provides information on the pathology, diagnosis, and treatment of a broad spectrum of renal diseases. Further information about renal diseases can be found in Barry M. Brenner and J. Michael Lazarus (eds.), *Acute Renal Failure*, 2nd ed. (1988); Barry M. Brenner and Floyd C. Rector, Jr. (eds.), *The Kidney*, 5th ed., 2 vol. (1996); Robert W. Schrier (ed.), *Renal and Electrolyte Disorders*, 6th ed. (2003); Stuart L. Stanton (ed.), *Clinical Gynecologic Urology* (1984); Donald W. Seldin and Gerhard Giebisch (eds.), *The Kidney: Physiology and Pathophysiology*, 3rd ed. (2000); and George L. Bakris, *The Kidney and Hypertension* (2004).

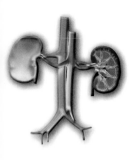

INDEX

A

abortions, 106–107
accelerated hypertension, 88
acid-base balance, regulation of, 61–64
acidosis, renal, 78, 112
acquired nephrogenic diabetes insipidus, 85
acute glomerulonephritis, 108
acute renal failure, 106–110
adrenal gland, 5, 36, 40, 57, 61, 138, 139
adrenocorticotropic hormone (ACTH), 36
advanced glycation end products, 125
aldosterone, 37, 40, 57, 61, 77, 120, 121
alkaptonuria, 69
Amanita phalloides, 108
amino acids, 45, 53, 63, 68, 69, 119, 122, 123, 126, 143, 161
amoxicillin, 102
ampicillin, 102
amyloidosis, renal, 111
analgesics, 102, 111
anemia, 32, 112, 113, 129, 137
aneurysms, 156
angiotensin, 33, 34, 38, 40, 120, 125
angiotensin-converting enzyme (ACE), 40

antibiotics, 102, 110, 118
antidiuretic hormones, 36, 84, 86–87
anuria, 89
arteriosclerosis, 88
arthritis, 69
artificial kidneys, 79, 110, 119, 141, 160–161
arylamines, 133, 136
asbestos, 137
atrial natriuretic peptide (ANP), 39–40
azathioprine, 157

B

Bartter, Frederic, 120
Bartter syndrome, 106, 119–122
bed-wetting, 96, 97
beetroot, 66
Bellini, ducts of, 7, 12–13
Bellini, Lorenzo, 142
bile salts, 60, 68
biological therapy, 136
biopsies, 93, 101, 131, 144, 149–150
birth defects, 133
blackwater fever, 68, 103
bladder cancer, 131, 132–136
blood transfusions, 68, 103, 107, 109

blue diaper syndrome, 126
bone disease, 113
Bowman's capsules, 9–10, 116
bradykinin, 38
Bright disease, 103, 106,
 114–117, 131
bulbourethral glands, 24

C

cadavers, 143, 157, 158, 159, 160
Candida, 100
carbamazepine, 87
carbonic anhydrase, 62
catecholamines, 38, 39, 40
catheters, 89, 90, 91, 92, 118,
 150, 156
central diabetes insipidus, 86
chemotherapy, 134, 135,
 138, 139
chronic renal failure, 110–114
ciprofloxacin, 102
cirrhosis, 68
"clean catch" technique, 152
clear cell renal cell carcinoma,
 139–140
Coccidioides, 100
colic, renal, 96
collagen, 4, 49, 88
coma, 87, 91, 112, 127
computed tomography (CT)
 scans, 101, 134, 138
constipation, 131
contraception, 98
coronary artery disease, 160

countercurrent exchange
 multiplication, 57
creatinine, 45, 48, 55, 76, 78,
 141, 148
creatinine clearance, 141,
 145, 148
crystalloids, 30, 49
cyclosporine, 157, 160
cystectomies, 135
cystinuria, 53, 69, 122
cystitis, 98
cystographies, 155
cystoscopes, 101, 131, 134,
 150–151

D

dehydration, 32, 43, 66, 77,
 80–84
desmopressin, 85, 86
De Toni-Fanconi syndrome,
 122–123
detrusor, 20, 25, 45, 46, 47, 70,
 71, 73, 90
diabetes, 53, 60, 64, 68, 84–86,
 88, 91, 99, 111, 115, 119,
 123–125, 131, 153
diabetic nephropathy, 115,
 123–125
dialysis, 110, 112, 114, 117, 137, 139,
 141, 157, 159, 160–163
diarrhea, 40, 43, 77, 80, 107, 100,
 112, 114, 128, 131
Diaz, Francisco, 150
dipstick tests, 101, 152, 153

diuresis, 59–60
diuretics, 85, 87, 117
dopamine, 38–39
ductus deferens, 17, 19
dwarfing, 130
dysuria, 91

E

edema, 76–77, 79, 109
elastin, 4
electrolytes, 30, 32, 34, 37, 43, 49,
   52, 61, 80, 83, 85, 109, 110,
   112, 121, 147
embryoma, 131, 136–137
endocrine glands, 37, 84
end-stage renal disease (ESRD),
   123, 124
Enterococcus, 100
enuresis, 96–97
epinephrine, 33
erythropoietic porphyria, 68
Escherichia coli, 100
estrogen, 37, 99, 102
excretion urography, 155

F

failure, renal, 43, 47, 78, 79, 83,
   89, 91, 98, 106–114, 117, 122,
   123, 127, 130, 139, 157, 160, 163
fallopian tubes, 135
flukes, 100, 103
food dyes, 66

G

Gitelman syndrome, 120, 121
glomerular filtration, 49–51, 144,
   145, 146

glomerulonephritis, 103, 106, 111,
   114–117, 148
glycopeptides, 49
glycosaminoglycans, 50, 51
gonorrhea, 94
gout, 94, 111, 153
granulomatous infiltration, 84
gynecologists, 151

H

heavy-metal poisoning, 108, 128
hematuria, 94, 102, 103–104, 153
hemodialysis, 142, 160
hemolysis, 68
hemorrhages, 35, 103, 106, 107,
   112, 116, 126, 127
heparin sulfate, 50
herpes, 100
Hippocrates, 151
hippurate, 60
hydrocortisone, 36–37
hydronephrosis, 92
hygiene, 100
hyperglycemia, 124
hyperplasia, 120
hypertension, 40, 77, 88, 89, 111,
   112, 113, 115, 117, 119, 124, 126,
   131, 146, 150, 153, 160
hypokalemia, 120
hypomagnesemia, 121
hyponatremia, 86
hypothalamus, 58, 59, 84, 85, 87

I

iminoglycinuria, 126
immunosuppressive drugs, 143,
   157, 158, 159, 160

immunotherapy, 136
incontinence, 46, 47, 91–92, 98
indomethacin, 122
insulin, 125
intoxication, water, 78
intravenous pyelography, 133
inulin clearance, 141, 145,
    148, 149
ischemia, 106, 108

J

jaundice, 68
juxtaglomerular apparatus, 14,
    34, 40, 89, 120

K

kallikrein, 38
ketones, 68, 152
kidney failure, 43, 47, 78, 79, 83,
    89, 91, 98, 106–114, 117, 122,
    123, 127, 130, 139, 157, 160, 163
kidney function tests, 147–148
kidneys and the renal system
    anatomy, 1–26
    cysts, 128–129, 140, 156
    development and function,
        27–43
    diseases and disorders, 5, 13,
        30, 37, 43, 51, 65, 66, 69,
        75–163
    stones, 91, 94, 95–96, 99, 103,
        122, 131, 150, 151, 154
    transplants, 32, 39, 93, 107, 108,
        114, 119, 130, 131, 141, 143,
        156–160
Kimmelstiel-Wilson disease, 115,
    123–125

kininogen, 38
Klebsiella, 100

L

lactosuria, 68
lithotriptors, 94
liver disease, 68
loop of Henle, 3, 8, 11–12, 49, 56,
    57, 61
low blood pressure, 128
Ludwig, Carl, 142

M

magnetic resonance imaging
    (MRI), 134, 138, 155, 156
malaria, 68, 103
malignant hypertension, 88
Malpighi, Marcello, 142
maple syrup urine disease, 69
metabolic alkalosis, 121
methionine malabsorption
    syndrome, 126
micturition, 45, 73–74, 90, 155
mineralocorticoids, 61
morphine, 59
Mycoplasma, 100

N

natriuretics, 39
necrosis, 106
nephrectomies, 139
nephritis, 76, 77, 93
nephroblastoma, 131, 136–137
nephrogenic diabetes insipidus,
    85, 86
nephrology, 141–143

nephropathy, 106, 123–125
nephrosclerosis, 126–127
nephrotic syndrome, 68, 79, 117, 128
neurophysin, 85
nicotine, 59
nitrofurantoin, 102
Nitze, Max, 150
nocturia, 91
norepinephrine, 33, 38, 40
nucleoproteins, 60

O

oasthouse urine disease, 126
obesity, 137
obstructive nephropathy, 92–94
oliguria, 89, 108, 109, 110
opiates, 87
orthostatic albuminuria, 68
osmolality, 77–78, 86, 87
osteodystrophy, renal, 129–130
ovaries, 135
overhydration, 32, 78

P

para-aminohippuric acid (PAH), 145–146
parasites, 13, 100, 103
parasympathetic nerves, 20, 71, 72, 74
passive incontinence, 47
pedicels, 50
penicillin, 60
peristaltic movement, 8, 17, 69
phenolsulfonphthalein (PSP) tests, 149

phenylketonuria, 69
pituitary gland, 36, 37, 58, 59, 60, 78, 84, 85, 87
podocytes, 50
polyuria, 91, 108
porphyrins, 68
potassium wasting syndrome, 106, 119–122
pregnancy, 41, 67, 75, 98, 118, 153
probenecid, 60
progesterone, 37
pronephros, 27–28
prostaglandins, 33, 37–38, 60, 121, 122
prostate, 19, 23, 29, 47, 92, 94, 99, 101, 131, 134, 135, 151, 154
proteinuria, 79, 117, 148
Proteus mirabilis, 100
proximal tubular reabsorption, 52–56
Pseudomonas, 100
pudendal nerves, 26, 72
pyelographies, 155
pyelonephritis, 103, 111, 114, 118–119, 148
pyridium, 102

Q

quantitative tests, 144–149

R

radiation, 93, 134, 135, 137, 138, 139, 155–156
radiation nephritis, 93
radioactive renograms, 155–156
renal cell carcinoma, 131, 137–140

renal function, evaluating, 143–150
renal plasma flow (RPF), 144, 146
renin, 14, 32, 33, 34, 38, 40, 89, 113, 120, 121
Richards, Alfred N., 142

S

sarcoidosis, 84
Scribner, Belding, 142
secondary hyperparathyroidism, 130
secretion mechanisms, 60–61
seizures, 87, 127
septicemia, 106
Serratia, 100
sexual intercourse, 98, 100, 102, 118
shock, 35, 80, 83, 93, 104, 106
Simon, Gustav, 151
smoking, 59, 133, 136, 137
somatic nerves, 26, 72
spinal disease, 69
Staphylococcus saprophyticus, 100
Starling, Ernest, 142
stones, kidney, 95–96, 99, 103, 154
strep throat, 115
strokes, 88
sulfonamides, 68, 102, 108
sulfonylureas, 125
sympathetic nerves, 6, 20, 38, 39, 71–72
syndrome of inappropriate antidiuretic hormone (SIADH), 86–87

T

tapeworms, 129
tetany, 76
thiazolidinediones, 125
threadworms, 100
thrombosis, renal vein, 128
transfusions, 68, 103, 107, 109
transplants, 32, 39, 93, 107, 108, 114, 119, 130, 131, 141, 143, 156–160, 164
transurethral resection, 134–135
trigone, 21, 70
tryptophan malabsorption syndrome, 126
tuberculosis, 84, 103, 111, 154
tuberous sclerosis, 137
tumours, 13, 37, 59, 75, 84, 87, 91, 94, 103, 104, 105, 129, 131, 136–137, 139, 140, 153, 154, 155, 156

U

ulcers, 103
ultrasound, 101, 138, 141, 155, 156
urea, 30, 41, 55, 65, 66, 76, 78, 83, 109, 112, 127, 161
uremia, 30, 110–114, 117, 119, 127, 130–131
uric acid, 45, 52, 60, 76, 111, 153
urinalysis, 138, 151, 152
urinary excretion, physiology of, 44–74
urinary function, evaluation of, 150–156

urinary tract infections (UTIs),
41, 98–102, 133, 153, 155
urine flow, disorders of, 89–94
urobilin, 66, 68
urochrome, 45, 66, 78
uroerythrin, 66
urogenital diaphragms, 24
urography, 114, 154–155
urology, 150–156
uroscopies, 151–152
urostomies, 135
uterus, 41, 134, 135

V

vascular disease, 88–89
vas deferens, 17, 19
vasopressin, 36, 38, 58, 59, 60, 78,
84, 85, 86, 87, 97, 146

viruses, 13, 100
vitamin D, 32, 37, 53, 112
voiding cystourethrograms
(VCUGs), 155
von Hippel-Lindau syndrome, 137

W

water deprivation tests,
146–147
water intoxication, 78
Wilms' tumour, 131, 136–137
Wolffian ducts, 3

X

X-rays, 101, 131, 134, 138, 139, 140,
151, 154–155